DOING IT RIGHT

Making the MOST
of Your Life

DOING IT RIGHT

Making the MOST
of Your Life

Dorothy Lapadula

SHAPOLSKY PUBLISHERS, INC.
NEW YORK

A Shapolsky Book

Copyright © 1990 by Dorothy Lapadula

For any additional information, contact:
Shapolsky Publishers, Inc.
136 West 22nd Street, New York, NY 10011
(212) 633-2022

1 2 3 4 5 6 7 8 9 10

Library of Congress Cataloging-in-Publication Data

Lapadula, Dorothy, 1933-
   Doing it right: making the most of your life.

   1. Women—Life skills guides. 2. Beauty, personal.
3. Self-actualization (psychology). I. Title.
HQ1221.L35   1990   646.7'0082   90-8541
ISBN 0-944007-57-0

Typeset by Woodmill Press, Somerville, NJ

Manufactured in the U.S.A.

*To my husband, Michael, without whom most
of the events in this book would never have taken
place, and to Cynthia and Missy, my favorite works of art*

CONTENTS

PREFACE

No, *Doing It Right* is not about sex. Well, maybe a little. It is about doing things for yourself and not depending on other people and other things—pills, machines and gadgets—to do them for you. It is about feeling good about yourself, and the only way that happens is when you are DOING IT RIGHT by yourself and for yourself.

Yes, the title, *Doing It Right*, is titillating. It's supposed to be. But I did not expect the reaction of the first literary agent I spoke to about it. When I told her the name of the book, she squealed, "Oooh, that's dirty!" The second agent I spoke to had another response: "Wow, what a great title!" Which only proves how different we are—all of us—in every way. One of the few things we all agree on is that we would like to change some part of our lives. Whether it is our job, our appearance or our interests, we can DO IT, and DOING IT ourselves, accomplishing it on our own, can be the most rewarding undertaking in our lifetime.

A good example of DOING IT RIGHT is this book. I've been toying with the idea of writing it for some time. Okay, so it's no *War and Peace*—but I did it. And that's what this is all about.

What makes me qualified to write about DOING IT RIGHT? The all too obvious answer would be that I have DONE IT RIGHT. But even though I have worked in the fields of art, advertising, interior design and fashion, that in itself does not endow me with the credentials to pontificate. However, when I was modeling in New York during high school and college years and then, after graduating, working in advertising and fashion, I did learn to Observe, Absorb, Digest and Retain everything that went on around me. Not just what was au courant, but rather who and what seemed always Right. Special. Cool. Perfect. I observed it in art through years of museum going, starting when I marked time in the Museum of Modern Art in New York between photography bookings as a teenager. One day the light bulb clicked on in my brain and I realized what the giants of art in this century were doing and why—and life has never been the same since. I'm still Observing, Absorbing and Enjoying art most, of all the wonders life offers, and with it I have learned that you enjoy nothing if you don't put something back into the bowl of wonders. And that, my darlings, is called DOING IT RIGHT.

Anything in the world that you want to do is possible. Change your job, take off weight, enrich your life, meet new people—you must start DOING IT RIGHT now. Thinking about it and talking about it (we are all so good about that) are O.K. if you are collecting ideas for a book or composing a piece of music, but for most of our goals, Immediacy—Doing It Now—is the only way to Do It. The skier will never get down the mountain if he or she doesn't push off at the top just as the swimmer will never reach the end of the pool if he or she doesn't dive into the water.

So dive in, push off—start DOING IT RIGHT now! You wouldn't have this book in your hand if you didn't want to Do Something different with your life or change something in it. Whether it's your hips, your friends or your interests that you want to change, start DOING IT RIGHT now—the minute you finish this hopefully short and not very sweet account.

And let me add here that all the opinions in this book are mine. Not the publisher's, not the editors'. All mine; whether it's white wine, black dresses, or what constitutes good taste or great style; the opinions are mine only and only mine.

CHAPTER I

HEY! WHATEVER HAPPENED TO EXCELLENCE?

Remember that word "excellence"? You're right. We almost never use it anymore and hardly ever have any reason to. Not many Oscar Wildes around anymore either. Oscar, you know, once spent a morning putting a comma in and an afternoon taking it out. Once in a while, though, we do run into people who have excellence as their goal. Let me tell you about a few I know.

We will start with a glowing example: Carol Aggar Fortas, my next-door neighbor in Georgetown and wife of the late Supreme Court Justice, Abe Fortas. Carol, who is a partner in the prestigious law firm of Arnold & Porter, has not only been DOING IT RIGHT way ahead of her time (she's had her law degree for fifty years), but she's also one of Washington's most colorful women. A great music lover (Abe played the violin and performed every Sunday evening with a distinguished group of not-very-amateur musicians), Carol still attends most performances of the National Symphony and the Washington Opera, as well as many other musical events at the Kennedy Center. At parties, she is always outstandingly dressed, which is a trick when you're under five feet tall. Usually, in one hand is a healthy glass of Jack Daniels and in the other a fine cigar. One January day, a year or so after we had moved into our house, I got out of a cab during the tail end of a snowstorm. Several inches had fallen since I had left in the morning for the Hirshhorn Museum and Sculpture Garden where I am a docent (giving tours and lectures on Twentieth Century art). In front of the Fortas house, I saw a young boy in a darling snowsuit, very similar to what my daughters had worn a few years before, even with the attached zippered hood. The boy was slinging the snow over his shoulder, shoveling furiously, never even lifting his head for a breather. I realized I'd better grab this little dynamo while I could to shovel our sidewalk and courtyard.

"Sonny," I yelled, "would you come over here to shovel when you're finished there?"

The small figure stopped shoveling, lifted its head, took the cigar out of its mouth and there stood Carol Fortas, distinguished jurist, early feminist, partner and tax expert in one of the greatest law firms in the land.

"Dorothy, you get out here and shovel the snow yourself. The air is great and the exercise is good for you!"

This order from a woman who had to be in her sixth decade at the time and who, then and now, swims every day of her life.(Obviously, shoveling snow is good for you only if you have been exercising all along.) What I especially like about this story is the punch line, which is that Carol had then and has now four live-in household helpers, including a driver-houseman. But she is Doing It her very best in every way, then, now and long before. Most women I know in similar circumstances (none as eminent, though) would have someone else shovel snow while they were driven to the health club to "exercise" or even better—wait at home for their "exercise person" to come and tell them how. O.K., that is better than not exercising at all. But thinking of it as a challenge, and Doing It yourself would also be fun, and a change from the routine. That's what make the difference between the Carols and the klutzes of the world. One is Doing It—and the other is Having It Done For Them.

The greatest dividend in Doing It your very best is the superb feeling of accomplishment that all the money and/or power in the world can't buy. Those Having It Done For Them will never know it unless they revamp their lifestyles and gear themselves toward Accomplishment and Excellence.

Another vignette that pops to mind regarding those lofty goals—Accomplishment and Excellence—has to do with the eminent heart surgeon, Dr. Michael DeBakey. Now we are really talking A and E!

I was returning from New York to Washington on the Metroliner, absolutely exhausted from a weekend of museum and gallery hopping and two nights of very late dinner dances. I was in the parlor car which had single seats you could swivel around to face one another, if you wished. I plopped into my assigned seat, swiveled the chair in front of me around and put my aching feet on that one. The car was only half-full and I figured on moving my feet fast if anyone claimed that chair. I, who normally wear a black eyeshade and can bear no noise in order to fall asleep, was in the arms of Morpheus before we left Penn Station.

Sometime later (technically, it was an hour and a half, because we were in Philadelphia), I heard the softest, deepest, Southern baritone voice saying, "I hate waking you, Miss, but this chair is the only one left . . . if you don't mind."

I looked up. "Why, Doctor DeBakey, what a surprise!" I delicately slid my size nines off his chair.

He was surprised that I recognized him (being as modest as he is Excellent and Accomplished), but his picture had been on the cover of *Time* magazine just two weeks before. Besides, Mike, my husband, who is a general surgeon, has always idolized Dr. DeBakey, who is, of course, the pioneer of heart surgery. Mike had told me how Dr. DeBakey rises at five in the morning to write papers and articles, then goes to the Methodist Hospital in Texas and performs four to six heart operations a day. He often returns to the hospital at night to check his patients again before going home.

So, I told the good heart doctor how my husband thought so highly of him—as did thousands of others, obviously—and how Mike would be thrilled to meet him, if he would agree to it, as Mike would be meeting the train. (He had flown back on the 7:00 a.m. shuttle.) Dr. DeBakey, in that beautiful, soft, Southern baritone allowed as how he would love to meet my husband.

Now, my Mike had never actually met DeBakey—just read everything he could about him and had, of course, read many of the articles he wrote for the medical journals. If I had just one picture in my lifetime that I wished I had taken it would be the one of Mike's face as I emerged from the train in Washington and said, "Oh, hi, Mike. I want you to meet someone . . . this is Doctor Michael DeBakey."

The most excellent thing the most Excellent heart doctor did then was to inquire about all of Mike's operations and ask all kinds of technical questions about medicine in the

Nation's Capital. Didn't dwell on what *he* was doing, not only in Texas but worldwide.

Somehow, being interested in what the other person is Doing is almost always a quality of the truly Excellent—the truly Accomplished.

It brings to mind a party at the National Gallery of Art where someone took a picture of Paul Mellon and me chatting about the glories of the British art which the party was celebrating. With my new book in mind, I asked him if it would be all right to use a picture that a photographer just snapped, in the book, fully aware that the Mellons frown deeply on publicity of any sort. And pictures . . . *jamais, jamais!* But, gallantly, as only a truly excellent gentleman of Mellon's stature could, he said, "Dorothy, I would be honored to have my picture in your book."

The irony of that little tale is that in the very ordinary world of today, where excellence is almost obsolete, a public relations person was "advising" me on the use of photographs in the book.

"They got to be celebs," he said, as I gave him a stack of pictures. "Bill Blass—O.K. Jim Garner—right. Mikhail Baryshnikov—oh, yeah! Paul Mellon—now, nobody knows this guy! What's he do again?"

The shocking fact is that if "nobody" translates as "Everyman," the P.R. man was probably right.

In the self-indulgent society of the eighties, a natural offspring of the notorious ME generation, instant gratification, instant recognition was IT. To take the time to learn about art or music that isn't immediately understood is too much like work. Not when people can flick on an empty, stupid, humorless sit-com and be instantly amused because the characters look and act like themselves.

Excellence certainly wasn't considered when they selected the marshal of the Rose Bowl Parade in 1988. Not that it was ever a position for an Einstein. But, they usually have a show-biz giant—Bob Hope, Gregory Peck or someone like that. In 1988, however, with criteria and taste plunging to the depths, a scruffy, TV sit-com person named Tony Danza was It! His only expertise seems to be a perfect pronunciation of the word "geez." Or, as he would say, "de *woid* geez." Incidentally, Danza also has a star on Hollywood Boulevard. Paul Newman doesn't. Neither does Meryl Streep.

May I ask it, please? Whatever happened to Excellence? Whatever happened to Taste and Style?

I know in the art world of New York why some of the hotshots like Julian Schnabel or Keith Haring can command astronomical prices and enjoy the excess of carefully planned publicity. It's all politics, aggressiveness, dealing, arranging, and exactly as Tom Wolfe wrote in *The Painted Word*. But, if you're Doing It in Art (or anything else), you learn about all these things and you never, ever buy a "hot shot" of the moment. Occasionally, you may stumble across one authentic artist among this group who decided to play the Agent-Gallery Owner-Critic game because it is so hard to be recognized any other way. Unfortunately, an artist is seldom judged on pure Excellence today but rather on how much hype can be conjured-up around him and how the number of nonknowledgeable new collectors is exploding. Many of the nouveau collectors go for older art (before the twentieth century), correctly figuring they can't go wrong with a proven master; or even a lesser master—at least they have stood the test of time. But, again, they almost always rely on the expertise of an art consultant, and, as in every field, there are those whose credentials are *not* excellent, as they should be, and whose appetites have been over-stimulated by the lifestyles of the nouveau clients. Being an art consultant myself, with the right credentials I hasten to add, I have seen too many collectors proudly displaying what are rather impressive-looking fake Bonnards, Picassos, and even a breathtaking Ver Meer. (Many of these forgers are fine artists; they have to be to occasionally fool even museum curators.) But, as in the instance of the faux Ver Meer, the art consultant should have known that this artist's lifetime output was very limited and most Ver Meers are in museums and the few that aren't grace the superlative collections of Queen Elizabeth of England and Baron H. H. Thyssen-Bornemisza in Switzerland. The consultant should know that without even looking it up. But the clients are usually in a hurry to acquire and the consultants (the unscrupulous ones) can't wait for the commissions.

That, *mes amis*, is when Excellence is never considered and no one is Doing It Right. The new collector should immerse himself in art history, spend a lot of free time in museums, be able to rely on his own taste and the style he wants to set in his collection. The feeling of accomplishment and satisfaction he or she would derive from Doing It the right way would give the collector more joy (or as much, anyway) than the art itself.

I know just one couple who have Done It exactly as described and their collection, like themselves, is smashing. They, too, started collecting the young, new, much-touted artists of the seventies and eighties. Then, after lots of observing and absorbing art at galleries, auctions and museums, they decided to take courses in art history and to take guided tours in museums as opposed to racing through on their own. They had found, as we all do, that racing through museums to "catch" the special shows was much like gulping down a meal and never even remembering what we ate or how it tasted. Now their exquisite collection of American Impressionists is backed with enormous exposure and knowledge of this school of art as well as others. I'm so proud of them because they were and are DOING IT with great taste and style in the particular field I'm so passionate about. When they stand before their superb Childe Hassam and discuss his flag paintings as opposed to his landscapes, I think my heart might burst!

Now, I know most of us can't go out and start collecting American Impressionists or any other major works of art. But we can start investigating, reading art history (and the texts in all those gorgeous "coffee table" art books), visiting museums, galleries and exhibitions. Discovering artists in your own community, talking to them and eventually starting to collect your favorites is just as exciting (well, almost) as going to an auction at Sotheby's and bidding on a Seurat.

It isn't only Art you can be passionate about, although in the long run the joys of it will probably outlast anything else. The study, the tracking and exploring is eternally rewarding. Anything you love—whether it's gardening, photography, skiing, horses—BE PASSIONATE. Love it, learn all you can about it and Do It and Keep Doing It well. That's Excellence!

Be like Lee Miller, the beautiful, blue-eyed blonde from Poughkeepsie, N.Y., who became a famous photographer after a lively liaison with the innovative American artist, Man Ray. Lee, who was only nineteen when she first saw the avant-garde work of Man Ray (even in Poughkeepsie, at nineteen, she was observing, absorbing, and Doing), raced down to Manhattan and tracked down the elusive artist in his studio. "I want to study with you. I want to learn everything you can teach me. I'll do anything in order to learn," Lee told him. Man Ray gazed at the lovely girl, who would become the first international artist's model, shook his head and said, "Sorry, but I'm leaving for Paris tomorrow." "No problem," (or words to that effect) answered Lee. "I'll go with you."

The rest, as they say in Paris, is *histoire*. But you know all about Man Ray—or you should after the socko show at the National Museum of American Art in 1988 and the equally excellent books and articles published in conjunction with the superb show. Born Emmanuel Radnitsky, Man Ray was a rebel who wore a bright red shirt to his high school graduation. He studied life drawing because he wanted to see a nude woman. He hung out at Alfred Stieglitz's gallery and there met Marcel Duchamp, the surrealist, whose *Nude Descending a Staircase* was the scandal of the landmark N.Y. Armory Show that formed the basis of the Rockefeller contemporary collection and later the Museum of Modern Art. Man Ray spoke no French, Duchamp no English, but they shared a sharp wit and great sense of fun. They played Dada tennis—without the net—the day they met. Duchamp convinced Man Ray to come to Paris, which he did and cut une grande swath in the art and intellectual circles after Duchamp introduced the "fiery elf" to the avant-garde. This was 1921. His surreal paintings and photographs dazzled. He embraced the Dada philosophy of destroying existing art forms and appealing to the arbitrary and absurd.

Man Ray made new use of the camera. His surreal photographs of haute couture in Paris, published in *Harper's* and *Vogue*, changed fashion photography from reality to

fantasy. The women he attracted were legend. Beyond
beautiful, they were clever, innovative, accomplished and,
most of all, original: Berenice Abbott, the photographer;
KiKi of Montparnasse, the gamine so lusted after by
Hemingway, Soutine and Utrillo; the fabulous Lee, who
broke Man Ray's heart when she left. She had learned her
lessons well, however, as witness her extraordinary
photographs. Like her mentor, she helped photography
inch toward a place in Art. Then, of course, came Juliet Man
Ray, the Martha Graham dancer he married. She is still
known—not as Mme. Ray or Mrs. Radnitsky—but rather as
Madame Man Ray.

What did this extraordinary artist have that earned him
such a high place in art as well as a top-ten rating among the
Legends of the Left Bank? Excellence, in everything he did.
For every great canvas, every exquisite photograph, there
were most likely innumerable rejects. Inventiveness, style
and great humor—qualities worth striving for. And all those
extraordinary BB's (beyond beautifuls)! How did a man
barely five feet in height with a stocky body and owlish
eyeglasses attract the BB's of the time? Aside from all that
talent, wit and sense of style, I'm told he had the world's
original pair of bedroom eyes. Whatever. Despite bouts of
depression, he was Doing It Surreally all his life, and that
almost obsolete word, Excellence, surely belonged to Man
Ray.

To get away from Art for a bit (I hate to and it won't be
completely, but we will still be talking Excellence). This
time, Excellence in direct opposition to Inadequacy. We
were at a dinner at the British Embassy about two years ago
to honor the outgoing chairman of the National Endowment of the Arts, Livingston Biddle. It was a very elegant

evening—black tie, of course, and all of the glitterati from
all the Arts in the United States were there plus a goodly
number of Brits. The conversation sparkled at every round
table of ten, as ours did with stories of Helen Hayes, George
Balanchine and Frank Stella. When the champagne was
served with dessert, Sir Oliver Wright, the ambassador from
Great Britain at the time, stepped up to the mike under a
portrait of Queen Elizabeth. Sir Oliver, who looks like the
leading man in a Noel Coward play and who spoke in the
dulcet tones we rejoice in when the great British actors
practice their art, went on about how important all the arts
are to the quality of our lives. (His delightful wife, Marjorie,
who trod the boards herself as a young actress-singer in
London, wowed all of Washington by appearing in many
amateur productions during their posting here.) Sir Oliver
then introduced Claiborne Pell of Rhode Island, the
patrician senator for whom Livingston Biddle worked and
who was responsible for pushing the National Endowment
of the Arts through Congress. In the senator's short tribute
to Biddle, the honoree, the unmistakable, upper-crust accent of the Brahmin he most certainly is cut through the
crowd as most people noticed how beautiful, clear and
similar to the great British voices Pell's is. Then, our first
chairman of the National Endowment of the Arts,
Livingston Biddle, rose to thank everyone for the honor
(and the presented plaque, of course). Now, Liv Biddle *is*
one of the Philadelphia Biddles but, please, don't confuse
this with anything like the "idle rich" cliché. He has been
working on Capitol Hill and writing books most of his life
when he wasn't racing about in World War II in Africa, Italy,
et al., driving an ambulance and performing outstanding
feats of bravery. (Very dashing he looks, too, in pictures

from those days in his beret and field togs.) Liv is still very dashing and has, as do his two predecessors that evening, an exceptionally mellifluous voice. After listening to the three of them, you felt you had just heard the three greatest orators of our time. Only Churchill was missing.

And, then, to the horror of almost everyone there, one of Washington, D.C.'s, elected officials got up to mumble a few words. And mumble away he did. I caught only two words of his embarrassing and inarticulate monologue—"proud" and "art." You can't hurt those too much. Someone at our table said, "Translation, please!"

Embarrassment, shame. After three articulate men who have been Doing It with taste and style all their lives and who *sound* it, there follows the horrendous example of someone who was given many opportunities in life and, as an elected official of Capital City, can't even speak well enough to be understood.

That evening stands out and always shall as the greatest example of Excellence and Achievement versus Inadequacy and Not Even Trying. (If my body is found in a pit after this, please recover!) Speaking of "bodies found" reminds me of another example of Excellence; one most of us hope we will never have reason to experience.

My husband and I were staying at the magnificent Hôtel du Cap in Cap d'Antibes, France, which is Everything Scott Fitzgerald and everyone else ever said about it. Elegance, beauty, style—those words don't even say enough. Excellence does.

One day, after walking down the long flower-bordered path from the great chateau to the sea, we noticed a young man being eased off his crutches into the sea by one of our all-time favorite characters, Professor Schnabel, the hotel's

swimming instructor. On a former visit to the glorious
hotel, we had noticed the small, discreet sign next to the
children's pool. It said, in English and French, of course:

> Professor Ignatz Schnabel
> Professeur des Arts Nautiques
> Premier Instructor of Swimming

In tiny letters beneath this declaration was the legend,
"formerly of the Fontainebleau Hotel, Miami." I don't
know why this sign always threw us into laughing fits, but it
did. It was probably after we saw the illustrious "professeur,"
who was out of Damon Runyon by way of Miami Beach,
which we had guessed even before the sighting. Very un-
Antibes was the good professor but right out of a thirties
movie version of "Miami Vice." Balding, stocky (could it
have been Man Ray, playing another Dada-surreal joke?)
with the cigar in his mouth, even in the water. For the most
part, he instructed children whose mothers or nannies
would sit around the borders of the pool, taking the sun
(topless, of course), while the professor would clap his
hands and yell, *"Très bien, mes enfants!"* or "Atta goil, baby!"
cigar still clamped between his teeth as he beamed at his
topless audience.

This day, however, he was very cautiously assisting the
handsome young man into the water and we watched as he
and the professor swam along together out to the raft about
a quarter mile out in the sea.

Later that evening, we were having a drink in the bar with
a lovely young girl we had met out on the same raft in the
afternoon. Nicole and I had formed an immediate alliance
because we were just about the only females at Eden Roc
who were not sunning or swimming topless, even though
she was French and more than qualified (as I must confess

I was, too). But some of us still feel that certain parts of our body are too private to display to the world at large. Nevertheless, we had a great time with the two other women who joined us on the raft that afternoon, sans tops, and carried on a conversation in French about New York with my husband, Mike, Nicole and me. After the first five minutes, it seemed perfectly natural. And, after all, Mike is a doctor. Our two topless raft mates would never make the cover of the *Sports Illustrated* swimsuit issue, as, like most heavy-set women, they were too large on top, as well as in all points south. A fellow we know said the funniest sight he had ever seen was the two, sans tops, diving off the board at Eden Roc, one after the other, as he was swimming along underneath. We are talking Surreal!

Anyway, Nicole, my young ally, suddenly jumped up that evening as the handsome fellow on crutches appeared. She introduced him and it turned out he was her husband and the son of the hotel's owner. They had just been married a few months, after one of the most harrowing kidnappings in recent times. The son, Paul, had been abducted the previous winter and held for ransom for several weeks. To transport him, his six-foot-three-inch body was folded in half and squeezed into a steamer trunk. This, of course, was the reason for the crutches. The kidnappers had broken both hips and Paul was spending every day of the summer swimming because, as he smilingly said, that was the only time he didn't feel the pain.

Mike gave Paul the name of the finest orthopedic surgeon in the world, in London, whose specialty was the replacement of hips. We learned later that Paul had both hips replaced and was doing well. I forget the amount of the ransom, but I do remember it was in the millions; the highest figure ever paid in a kidnapping case. And, oh yes, the kidnappers were never caught.

What I remember most of all was Paul, who looks like a young Peter Duchin, and his upbeat, inspiring, optimistic attitude. He laughed more at the tale of our topless raft mates than we did and at his own snaring away of le professeur Schnabel from his captive audience at the kiddie pool. Excellence, Doing It Right; that's what it is all about. And that's what Paul is all about. We don't ever want excellence to slip away altogether and it won't—as long as there are any Pauls around.

As a matter of fact, as long as we have people in our world like the Reverend William Byron, S.J., president of the Catholic University of America, we are in good hands. He asks students a key question, "Which is more important to you, your credit card or your library card?" V-E-R-Y KEY! I know how much pleasure, knowledge, and joy my library cards have brought me since I've been a very little girl. Anyone who doesn't use libraries is missing one of the greatest slices of the Pie of Life. No matter how many books you have at home, and we have hundreds, you can't ever have enough.

When we first moved into our house in Washington, I was telling someone how wonderful it was; built in 1796 as a typically Georgian house, then added to and remodeled in the thirties by one of America's foremost architects, W. Burell Hoffman. He had turned it into a replica of the then-diplomat owner's former home in France. Marble staircase, sixteen-foot ceilings, courtyard, garden, et al. And, I added, a great bonus was that the Georgetown Library was two doors away, on the corner!

"Oh," replied my acquaintance, "as if you would ever use that!"

Obviously, she was (is) one of the legion of the poor, starving souls that Auntie Mame referred to who never even approach the Feast that life offers. Anyway, the good Father Byron, when he asks that key question of his students is challenging them on their commitment to the life of the mind.

"This is the generation that made 'party' a verb," he says. They can't solve the world-wide problems unless they develop their intellects now. "It is heresy," (we certainly don't hear that term anymore!) Father Byron notes, "to say what you do is what you are, or what you have is what you are." You are whatever is stored in the intellect—the mind—and how you *use* it.

"Right on," we hope the students are saying and Doing. Because Father Byron is committed to building Excellence.

Perhaps we started losing this thing called Excellence soon after World War II. We were flush with victory and everything was Easy. That particular generation who fought in the war and grew up in the Depression seems to have had one philosophy: when they had children, those children would never want for anything, never have to work hard (as did many of their parents) and, in general, never have to Strive. We all want the best for our children, but I do believe that generation of parents harmed their children by giving them anything they wanted and rarely setting important goals for them. Taking away incentive is like robbing one of life.

As a consequence, we have legions of over-age hippies in their thirties and forties who, armed with college degrees (their parents made sure of that), are not working much;

they never wanted to sit at a desk, and I suppose they never will. If they are working, it's usually at some menial job.

Needless to say, it's a bad situation; a far, far cry from Excellence. So we are hoping that the generation now partially in Father Byron's hands and others like him will strive for the Excellence once synonymous with America.

I remember being somewhat involved with the aging hippie syndrome. Fired up by Ralph Nader's Righting the World in the early seventies, I volunteered to Serve! The only opening the sincere but sometimes abrasive Ralph had at the time was in his tax-reform group. Not particularly interested in that reform, I was, however, fascinated by the group itself. Heading it was a fine young, serious tax lawyer, a replica of big Ralph. His assistant and editor of our tax-reform newsletter, which I was assigned to write articles for, was a Woody Allen clone—and almost as funny. But, what fascinated me most (remember, I had been a teenage model in New York and, later, a fashion executive) were the three female lawyers who were not only hippies but Dirty Hippies. I was involved with the group over a couple of years and I would take an oath that none of those three heads had ever been shampooed. Also, even though I was very careful to wear my most scruffy outfits to the office, I couldn't even squeeze into their league. I refused to tear holes in the knees of my jeans, my sweaters were cleaned now and then, and my blouses would be washed and pressed. Even though I wore no makeup—all right, maybe a trace of lipstick—and tried to be outraged and sincere at all times, I just couldn't be pals with these "gals." Josh, however, the Woody-Allen type, and I had a hilarious time reading and answering tax-reform letters to the editor (that was Josh), and then, what we would *really* like to tell these people. The reasons many people offered for not paying taxes were so self-serving and bizarre they were ludicrous. We would yell our hypothetical answers across the room to each other while the three overly serious, humorless feminist lawyers glared at us.

After a couple of years, much as I admired what Ralph Nader is and was trying to do, I had had enough. What really turned me off was when the three women would take their lunch, usually sent in from a nearby Capitol Hill restaurant, and place it on the floor where they would sit down and eat it. Josh and I, at each end of the room, would have to look at their backs, their clotted hair and, worst of all, the flabs of skin between their too-small children's sweaters—radical chic in the early seventies—and their torn jeans.

Now, the lady lawyers could have gone out for lunch since it cost more to have it sent in or, at least, eaten at their desks. But, no, these options were not bizarre enough. The almost daily picnic did me in. A strange example of how someone, in this case Ralph Nader, striving always for Excellence could be surrounded by inadequacy, however technically qualified.

There is always a bit of humor in everything we do. When the tax-reform group marched on the Nixon White House with placards on sticks, a *Washington Post* photographer took our picture. Guess where that picture landed? Front page center, the next morning. My father called me from New York and said, "I can't believe you are doing this and whatever was that that you were wearing?" It was one of my most sincere hippie outfits . . . with a rebel cap, of course! A couple of years before, when I was in Moscow, where my ex-husband was serving as an army attaché, my father had written for me to please send a picture as he hadn't seen me in almost two years. The only one I had happened to be quite good, except that in it I was trying to smoke a cigar. He didn't like that one any more than my march on the White House. At least, in each instance, I was Doing It!

As a finale in our quest for Excellence, I can offer no better example than when the United States sent W. Edwards Deming, one of our greatest statisticians, to work with Japanese industry after World War II to improve their quality. (He certainly did that!) Japan is so grateful that they award a Deming Prize annually to the Japanese firms who demonstrate the greatest increase in Quality!

Why did we let Deming get away? Can we capture the Excellence he taught the Japanese? And, especially, the Spirit that sent him there?

We hope so. We think so. We know so. All we have to do is start Doing It Right again—our very best, right now!

CHAPTER II

YOU CAN'T BE TOO RICH . . .
BUT YOU *CAN* BE TOO THIN

Yes! You can be too thin. It *is* hard to believe if you are waging a constant battle with weight and bulges. But, then, maybe you have been cheating on one diet after another and skipping your exercise. Maybe. But just for a minute picture our former first lady, Nancy Reagan, with ten or more pounds on her body. As attractive as she certainly is now, her cheeks would fill out just a little as would the rest of her body and, believe me, she would look ten years younger. I have seen two women I know who were borderline anorexics—lunching and sometimes dining on Perrier, lettuce and black coffee—finally start eating sensibly. The change is *extraordinary*. Each one of them looks a decade younger than before. Which proves that for each pound you are seriously underweight, you add one year to your appearance. They are both looking and, thankfully, acting sweeter, softer and happier than they have for years. Along with all the weight, they had lost good skin tone (more than wrinkles, a dead giveaway of aging), sparkling eyes and shining hair. To say nothing of sunny dispositions, energy, interests and things like that. But now they are back to normal, thankfully, with those CRUCIAL ten or twelve pounds. I am emphasizing "too thin" because dieting has become such an obsession in the last twenty years that many people I know, most of whom were all of average weight at one time, are way beyond slim, trim and attractive. They are mostly, or look like, borderline anorexics. One acquaintance, whom I hadn't seen in a couple of months, was across the room at a party. Someone next to me said, "Oh, that must be Judy's mother—looks just like her." As the woman inched over to us, we said in unison, "Oh, my God, that's Judy, not her mother!" An identical case, only involving a male diet-freak, happened soon after—several people thought it was the man's older brother. After forty, you must *remember this:* for every pound underweight, you add a year to your age.

So don't be excessive. If you have a problem with your bod, start taking it off or building it up in MODERATION. But start Doing It and keep Doing It. Now!

How you look *does* determine how people react to you. It is true that we should be more concerned with what people are really like—their character and personality—but it is appearance that we do react to immediately. Few of us continue to admire anyone who looks good but proves to be a big zero. On the other hand, we have many examples of some great "lookers" with no other noticeable pluses married to super partners. They may be exceptions but it does prove that appearance counts.

So start Doing It Right about your appearance right now.

Stand in front of a full-length mirror. Be honest. Analyze. If your waist is too thick, your tummy too noticeable or your thighs and buttocks too fleshy—don't give up. They are the most common flaws and the easiest to correct if you just start Doing It Now! You don't have to search for exercise classes to fit your schedule and your budget. I know many women who fill their weeks and years with these classes and I can honestly say, in most cases, there are no noticeable results; the classes are used as time-fillers. The movie-star tapes are a "must have" status symbol for many women. They buy them and use them a few times, if at all. What they really Do is talk about them. A lot.

It's true that it is much more enjoyable to exercise to music so I recommend putting on one of the rock music stations, even if you prefer Brahms, because our bodies naturally respond to the rhythmic beat of that brute music even if our ears do not. And we move more parts. When you have that energizing music going, you're ready to start Doing It.

The Tummy. Most of us who are, as the French say, "of a certain age," or as Vera Charles of *Auntie Mame* fame put it, "somewhere between forty and death," need to flatten this pro-trusion. The abdomen does have a natural curve to it but we don't want that curve extending into infinity. There are many gadgets and machines on the market to supposedly reduce the tummy with very little effort on your part, but you don't need those any more than you need to sign away part of your life and income to an exercise class. What you have to Do is to make up your mind to get rid of that tennis ball, that grapefruit or that watermelon you refer to as your tummy. You must vow to do this one exercise at least five times a week. After a while, two or three times a week is enough because you will have strengthened those flabby, weak, least used muscles of the abdomen. The result will be stunning.

Here you go—you're DOING IT RIGHT. You're on the floor. You *need* that hard floor for good results. You don't need an exercise mat, a flat carpet with a beach towel over it is fine. Lie perfectly flat with your hands palms down at your sides. Slowly bend your knees and bring your legs up as close to your face as possible. Then stretch your legs out and as high as you can into the air. Now comes the clincher, and this *will* clinch if you're not in shape. Slowly, as slowly as you have ever done anything in your life, lower those limbs—knees together legs perfectly straight—S-L-O-W-L-Y to the floor. It is going to hurt, your eyes are going to smart, you may even cry. But something so positive is going to happen to you that if you do cry, you'll be shedding tears of joy. You'll actually feel an abdominal muscle or two groan with delight at being given Something To Do! Now Do It once or twice more—the first day. It should and will probably feel sore in your lower regions for a day or so. That's perfectly normal since you haven't been using those muscles for years—if ever. Then skip a day and get down on the floor again and repeat the exercise. *Remember, it is how slowly you lower your legs that is important.* You will feel the muscle tug on the second round but not as much as during the initial bout. You will always feel a slight contraction there in the abdomen. Expect it and enjoy it because you know what you are DOING is working. Build up gradually from two, three or four a day until you do the exercise about fifteen to twenty times. It is a workout but not an unpleasant one with music or the TV on. The results are so sensational you'll never give it up. Also, you don't have to shift positions, drag out machines and do a complicated routine. This one does it ALL, so deep-six all the extraneous material. This exercise is your lifetime guarantee to a Flat Tummy!

If you suffer from spreading hips and/or bulging buttocks, the following exercise which I call the "Bang-Bang" is for you. Again, that hard floor is almost as beneficial as the exercise itself. (Oh, how the expensive exercise machine manufacturers are going to hate me for this!) A very thin rug or towel is allowed. Now, in a sitting position, with both hands pressed hard to the floor in back of you, arms straight, lift your body slightly up off the floor turning a bit to the right and then *bang* the right hip down onto the floor. Then twist slightly to the left hip and *bang* that one down as hard as you can. The point of this simple but effective "Bang-Bang" is hitting those hips and cheeks as hard and as often as you can. Obviously, they will stop spreading and extending. And if they have already done so, they will be forced to flatten down with all that pounding. The "Bang-Bang" will leave you a bit sore at first but, again, the results are so gratifying you'll soon be banging away to "60 Minutes" or Lionel Ritchie. The point is to bang-bang 'til you can't lift off the floor, pause, then bang away again. A total of fifteen to twenty minutes a day of "Bang-Bang" is necessary if you're spreading and extending, but, like the tummy flattener it is the only exercise you will have to do in the hip and buttock department if you have a problem in those locations. So start Doing It Now. You're going to love to "Bang-Bang"!

The last, but in most cases not the least, of our Big Three body problems is the waistline. Here the excesses of our appetites gather and cluster like nowhere else on the body. But it is just as easy to keep it off or take it off if you start Doing It Right now. Right Now. For instance, if you have had any supremely fattening goodies today, like fettucine alfredo, a hot fudge sundae, a couple of pina coladas—jump up right now and stand with your arms raised over your head and your feet a few inches apart. Twist to your left and, keeping your knees straight, touch your left heel with your right hand. Then straighten up to the first position with your arms out high over your head and twist to your right and touch your right heel with your left hand, then back to the first position. Now, you might not make it all the way down to your heel with your hand at first but you will be bending and twisting that waist of yours, making it impossible for a micro-morsel of fat to gather there. This is probably the oldest and most effective waistline exercise in the world. If there's a waistline exercise cliché, this is it 'cause it always works. If there's an Old Testament of Exercises, it must begin with this one because it's the TRUE WAY to take the fat off or keep it from gathering. Call it the Bend and Twist. No matter how tired you are—Do It and Keep Doing It the rest of your life. Begin with ten or so bends to each side and work up to fifty; eventually 100 B&Ts. You'll be so glad you're Doing It, especially knowing you can have a couple of chocolates or anything else as long as you know there's a way to keep the formerly Forbidden Delights from showing. Remember: when you are twisting and bending (it gets to FEEL so good), you are also burning calories like mad. Just about as many as swimming, which is the best sports exercise, and you are moving about the same number of parts. Almost.

You can do all of the Big Three if you have problems in each department or just concentrate on the one where you do. I recommend though that you do the Bend and Twist whether you have problems at the waistline or not. It will keep problems from ever forming there and it will really make you feel wonderful. Most of us can't play tennis every day but this exercise will make you feel as fit as if you've played a few sets. Also, exercise-wise, the Bend and Twist is more beneficial because it concentrates on one specific area. So, come on, start Doing It. You're going to see and feel the Difference in a very short time!

I have zeroed in on the areas where most of us have figure problems. If you do all the exercises three or four times a week the rest of your life—yes, the rest of your life—they become as much a part of your routine as brushing your teeth. You will reap the benefits of a firm, slim body and you will not only look great but you will feel marvelous. In most cases, you will be exercising the least used parts of your body. You know what happens to cars and other machines that are not put to use. So start Doing It! Don't rust away with inactivity and indecision. Start Doing It Now!

While we are talking about How We Look, we obviously can't ignore Diet. So much has been written about what we eat that it would be redundant of me to repeat all the information we have been given in the last twenty years. The food section of your newspaper has countless articles on diet every week. So, of course, do most of the monthly magazines. And the books that are written on the subject are innumerable. Opinions vary and each diet offered differs in one way or another. The one element every diet author alive agrees on is that the number one culprit in our diets is fat. FAT. It even sounds disgusting! If you are ten to twenty pounds overweight—which is about average—you can easily take that weight off and keep it off the rest of your life. It is a matter of routine, just as the exercises are. But, again you must start Doing It!

What you must start Doing at your very next meal—be it breakfast, lunch or dinner—is eat half or less of everything you usually have at that meal. If you weigh over ten pounds too much, I would cut it to a third of what you usually eat. And if you want to lose ten of those twenty pounds faster— you can eat very nutritious, filling meals if you just count calories and keep the calories under 1,000 a day, preferably about 800—you will drop those first ten pounds in about ten days. I won't include a calorie counter here because if you don't know the approximate calories in most foods by now, then you are not serious about losing that weight. (You can always buy a little calorie counter in the supermarket if you want to be that exacting.)

I'll give you an approximately 800-calorie-a-day menu, just in case you haven't looked at a magazine or newspaper in the last few years. (Don't laugh. Gore Vidal says eighty-two percent of us don't read newspapers.) Remember, this is approximate. You don't have to be on the button with every single calorie you consume.

Breakfast. Don't skip it. You'll eat twice as much for lunch if you do. Have a medium-sized orange. I know it is quicker and easier to gulp down a glass of juice but it is far more nutritious with all that fiber in the pulp to eat it whole. And, not incidentally, much more filling. It would be hard to find a more beneficial food that tastes as good as a fresh, sweet orange. So, even if you don't have one to start your day, be sure to include an orange at some other point later on. Only eighty calories, too.

Then have a slice of thin bread or toast. There are many delicious, thin-sliced breads available today and just one slice is only forty calories. You can put a smidgen of butter or jam on it—just a mere film—and it will only be about sixty calories total.

You can also have a very small bowl of hot or cold cereal; approximately two or three tablespoons of oatmeal or a bran cereal with a half teaspoon of sugar and a dash of skim milk or even low-fat milk (at these piddling amounts, you can go for the better taste). That will only add up to another eighty cals. Go ahead and have your coffee or tea, again with a half teaspoon of sugar and a whole teaspoon of cream or whole milk. For those infinitesimal number of calories, eight for the sugar and twenty for the cream or milk, you can make it something to look forward to rather than dread. Now our total count for breakfast is only about two hundred and fifty calories, counting the whole orange. O.K., now you're Doing It!

Before we go on to Lunch, let me say a few words about cholesterol and fats. While I am not a nutritionist, I have read a great deal about foods and their content and especially about those two culprits, cholesterol and fat. I agree with my husband, who is a doctor, that moderation in everything is the key to a healthier life. He feels that many people—food writers   included—have gone overboard on the cholesterol-fat debate. Of course, too much of either rascal in your diet will most likely take its toll. The arteries will probably clog up and then you're in trouble. However, everyone should have their cholesterol level checked (a very simple test) and, if it is anywhere above normal, that's when you should be very careful of what you eat. But so many sheep (oops, I mean people) just follow the line of the day and, without ever being checked, never look an egg in the yolk again. Or they cry out in horror if someone has Eggs Benedict for brunch. Or they scowl when you order ice cream and usually deliver a sermon on the "evils of" as they down their sorbet. MODERATION! Have they ever heard, of it? No one in their right mind would eat Eggs Benedict more than once or twice a fortnight, ice cream likewise. If, however, you are DOING IT RIGHT—maintaining your weight, doing your exercises three times a week, and your cholesterol level is low or normal—you can have your ice cream or any other Forbidden Food as long as you don't exceed three teaspoons of it at any time. Remember, if you're serious about DOING IT—maintaining that svelte bod—you are always going to have one six-letter word etched in your brain. The word is "AMOUNT" and using it in every food encounter for the rest of your life will make the difference in how you look and especially how you feel about yourself. You can resign yourself to the fact that ice cream (or any other goodie) is forbidden, *but* if you're really Doing It, you can go to the kitchen right now and have a teaspoon or two. You just have to constantly remember the *amount* is most important and, of course, click away the calorie count on your mental register. Back to . . .

Lunch. This, of course, is the 800-calorie-a-day menu for those of you who want to drop ten to twenty pounds. Seriously.

If you have had your cholesterol level tested and it is either low or normal, you know that for a short period of time two or three eggs a day will not harm you. I'm pushing the egg because, like the orange, it is loaded with nutrients, mainly protein. It is delicious and very low in cals, only sixty-five for a medium-size egg. Just one hard-boiled egg is the most filling, satisfying food of all. Yes, a Little salt and pepper is allowed. A Little almost anything is allowed, because we are not fanatics and because we are very into that six-letter word AMOUNT, in everything we eat. So we have two hard-boiled eggs for our diet lunch with a whole tomato, a slice of very thin bread with a trace of apple butter or jelly (repeat, a TRACE), and either coffee, tea or a small glass of juice or fat-free milk. By small, I mean three or four ounces. Remember, you are on a quick-loss diet and just a taste or trace of something should be a treat. O.K. That's about 270 cals and combined with breakfast we are only up to 520. That leaves approximately 280 calories for dinner. Make it an even 300 left—the extra twenty won't matter at all.

All right—you are Doing It Right. You are on this two-week, quick-loss diet and you have social obligations like all of us. But unlike most of us, you are *not* going to Talk About Your Diet. Please. You can stay home and hide from a social life to avoid temptation but that only proves you a coward. It is much more positive to go and ignore the tempting food and munch on celery or carrots (filling and not enough calories to count) and have your glass or two of club soda with a lime or lemon (no count there, either). You will feel absolutely wonderful that you have this top-secret secret (your diet) and that you are really Doing It—losing weight while you are eating, drinking and having fun at a party. Do me one favor though, even when you are not on the diet: don't order white wine or Perrier. Both have become such clichés and in any honest taste test a good club soda registers way above the ubiquitous Perrier. And I must admit I have a personal vendetta about white wine. After years of being served sour, acidic, vinegar-like substances at embassies, gallery openings, and parties, I cringe when someone actually orders it. There is some fabulous vintage white wine out there, but you are *never* served it when you simply order you-know-what. Also, all that acid in your tummy is far worse for you than any mixed drink. I must say I agree with Bette Davis, who said she cringes when a Real "man-looking man" orders white wine. She means, naturally, he doesn't have to order a boilermaker or a couple of shooters in order to be a Real Guy. But a little whiskey and soda, or even a little soda, is less effete than white wine. I guess it's because I hate clichés. European women often order juice or Dubonnet, but, alas, many American women are sheep-like and white wine (I hate even saying it) is the drink of the times, as was Kir before that. A few years ago, when I was a partner in an art gallery in Georgetown, I was so tired of going to other gallery openings and never being able to order anything but—you guessed it—white wine that I insisted we have Real Drinks even if I had to supply them myself, which I did to the grateful satisfaction of an array of art lovers. As for the calories, a third of a jigger of scotch or bourbon with soda or water adds up to about thirty calories. I know that's a weak drink but it is very satisfying and extremely easy to enjoy. After a few evenings of these very light drinks you won't be able to look at a strong one. Whenever I'm served a dark brown drink after I have ordered a very light one, I send it back until it arrives at just the right color. Which is, if you'll excuse the expression, the color of—you guessed it—white wine!

All right. You are Doing It. Keeping up with your social obligations while you're on the quick-loss diet. Whether you are out or at home you have about three hundred calories to spend on your . . .

Dinner. You can have a small, lean piece of broiled chicken or fish; mounds of spinach, broccoli, carrots or almost any other veggie, with the exception of peas, corn or lima beans; lettuce and tomato salad sprinkled with raw carrots and celery and topped with a teaspoon of low-cal dressing. Have a short glass of low-fat milk or coffee or tea with a teaspoon of milk and a half teaspoon of sugar.

Dessert? Yes, you CAN have dessert. But save it 'til later in the evening. It's always nice to have a treat to look forward to. And the treat can vary. You can have a few teaspoons of jello (we forget how sweet and filling it is) or a few slices of any fruit or, once in a while, a hard candy. Remember, you are still on the quick-loss diet—so these are little dividends for your good behavior all day.

O.K., you *are* Doing It Right. You have charged through your first day of the quick-loss diet (from here on we will refer to it simply as the QLD) and you are feeling thinner already. There's a lot to be said for Cary Grant's old axiom, "Think thin." If you are really watching your diet and are seriously doing your exercises, you will find it very easy to think thin. It is absolutely impossible to feel thin when you nibble all day and sit and watch sports (people exercising) or anything else on TV instead of getting out there and exercising yourself. You'll be pleasantly surprised at how thin you will feel if you are watching your diet and exercising. When you have fifteen or twenty minutes to spare either at home or at the office get out and take a brisk walk. No, you don't have to jog. Health experts are now finding what most people with any common sense knew all along: that a long, brisk walk is just as beneficial as jogging. In fact, more so. The biggest plus is that you don't have to change into those awful outfits with matching headbands and "beyond hideous" sneakers! You will find that when you are Doing It—making these routines part of your daily life—you will not only think thin and feel thin, you will BE THIN because you are actively working at it all the time.

Once you have lost the ten to twenty pounds on the QLD, you will, of course, continue doing your exercises three or four times a week and as many sports as you enjoy, even if it is only long, brisk (that word even makes you feel good) walks. Also, although it may sound silly, you can make a beneficial exercise out of almost everything you do. When you make a bed, for instance, stretch across it to straighten the sheets; twist, turn and reach out as you plump the pillows; bend forward and back as you pull the bedspread. Swing your arms around in rotating circles when you finish. You will not only have made the bed but also have taken what should be a daily step in keeping the body beautiful. This will probably sound even sillier—but the results are anything but. When you are by yourself, put on some music with a good fast beat and dance. Dance wildly to the beat, moving as many parts of the body as you can; pulling and stretching where you can feel it trimming you down. It's fun and, as you know, there's no such thing as a fat dancer. Another little something to add to your repertoire of THIN TRICKS is to purposely leave something upstairs or down, a few times a day, so you will have to make repeat trips. This is great for the legs, for burning up calories and super for that muscle called the Heart. These are just a few THIN TRICKS that take very few minutes each day, but add them to your regular exercises and your diet-watching and you will be thinking thinner than Cary G. ever imagined.

You may wonder why I feel qualified to be any sort of authority on the subject of weight control or diet. For the simple reason that everything I have told you has worked for me for over thirty years. I am the exact same weight now as I was at fourteen years of age and, even more significant, the measurements are exactly the same. That also includes five full-term pregnancies. The question I've been asked most often is "How do you stay so trim?" Usually asked by someone really out of shape and, most often, answered by themselves to the tune of "Oh, you're one of those lucky ones—born thin—you never have to diet or exercise." They answer it that way because that is what they would like to believe. To wit, that it is next to impossible for them (so they compensate by eating too often and/or too much) and easy for the rest of us who were lucky enough to be born with slim forebears. They obviously don't know about Doing It Right: doing those exercises religiously and leaving some food on your plate at every meal for the rest of your life. NFA, or Never Finish Anything, is the other rule you will live by the rest of your life.

Let me tell you how NFA became a rule of life under rather extraordinary conditions. A little more than twenty years ago I spent two years living in the American Embassy in Moscow, where my former husband was one of the military attachés. Dreary as that may sound, they were two of the most exciting, rewarding years I have ever experienced. We could not, of course, socialize with our Soviet counterparts as you do with your host country's citizens in a non-Iron Curtain country. But socialize we did with our diplomatic counterparts from "friendly" nations. There were luncheons, receptions, cocktail parties and formal dinners daily (except Sundays), and often two or three functions a day. There were over 150 embassies in Moscow. As in any other capital, including Washington, D.C., each embassy had its National Day; its Army Day; its visiting V.I.P.s. Each event was celebrated with a spectacular party.

The luncheons were five courses with three wines. The receptions always featured mounds of Beluga caviar surrounded by other irresistible delicacies. Incidentally, the diplomatic stores in Moscow are the only places in which you can buy caviar and you must be a foreign diplomat to even approach the stores. Many people think that Soviet citizens can walk into any supermarket and buy all the caviar they want. Wrong. There's no caviar at all for them to buy. In fact, there are no supermarkets. But I digress. After the receptions, sometimes two in one evening, there was always a formal dinner consisting of a seven-course meal served with four or five wines. With the American military in formal dress, along with the military of other countries, their gold braid and the scarlet-lined capes of the British Navy flashing, and the women, in many cases, equally dazzling, it made for rather heady evenings. And yet, after awhile, four or five heady evenings a week became too much of a good thing. The endless extended dinners, added to the ritual daily luncheons, extended many a waistline in the diplomatic service. I mention this only to illustrate a point. When we were leaving the embassy after our tour of duty was finished, and at yet another round of farewell parties, someone asked me how I had "kept my figure" during our two-year stint. I replied that long ago I realized there was only one way to survive: take just a couple of sips of soup; a forkful of fish; lots of the veggies; a forkful or two of meat and a spoonful or two of dessert; a sip or two of the wines (only in the evening) and a half a glass of champagne, which I really enjoy. In other words, it was the birth of my NFA theory, which I have employed successfully ever since. And you will too, once you start Doing It Right. It will become a life-long habit—the discipline of exercise and the

AMOUNT of foods you eat. As I have mentioned before, the greatest feeling of all, after you have shed those pounds and whittled away the bulges, is how good you will feel about yourself. And that, of course, will encourage you to keep Doing It Right the rest of your life.

CHAPTER III

"THE WAY YOU WEAR YOUR HAT"
(and Everything Else)

Most of us don't wear hats anymore. Yes, the Helen Hokinson ladies of the thirties and forties in their stilted, contrived little hats made the *New Yorker* cartoons funny, even without the captions. But today's casual, unconstructed fashions would be even funnier than the Hokinson cartoons if we wore what I call "hat hats." However, every outfit you wear, whether it's jeans and a sweater or a ball gown, looks finished—more complete—with something "related" on your head. It can be a scarf, a cap, a ribbon, a headband, a flower. It is how you wear it—where you place it—that makes the difference. A few years ago, an attractive divorcee I know was followed for several blocks in Paris by a man she had noticed as she left the lobby of the Ritz Hotel. She noticed him because he was a very attractive, well-known actor. She was going to the hairdresser wearing a red Chanel suit and a two-inch-high crested red beret which she had bought at a hat bar in Bonwit Teller. It sounds impossible but when she emerged from the hairdresser there

The chapter title is from the Gershwins' "They Can't Take That Away from Me."

waiting for her was the well-known actor with a somewhat
puzzled look on his face. She will never forget what he said.
"I know this is ridiculous, but the way you wear that hat.
Could you put it on for me again and allow me to take you
to lunch?" Thus the beginning of a beautiful relationship.
O.K., she was Miss Philadelphia twenty years before and still
looked every bit as good. All right, she was wearing a Chanel
suit but it could just as well have been a Chanel knock-off
or any classically cut red suit. The "hat-bar" hat, however,
was the trigger. If you think that encounter would have
happened if the same woman was wearing a basic black suit
minus the hat then you had better get down to some serious
reading of this chapter. P.S.: That beret was not a flat one,
which is flattering to no one except possibly a Basque
fisherman, but rather a beret-type hat raised in front a
couple of inches—and spelling instant chic.

Burying Black and Other Clichés

First of all, Basic Black is the cliché of the fashion industry. When Chanel back in the Twenties came up with
the Little Black Dress, it was the farthest cry from how ninety
percent of women have translated the black dress ever since.
Chanel's LBD was cut beautifully and almost always accented with tons of real, but mostly faux, jewelry—especially
long, white pearls and gold chains—and, usually, white
collar and cuffs. Why the accents? Because all that white is
flattering to everyone and the LBD with no "lighting," no
accent, is about as flattering as a funeral shroud. There are
exceptions, of course. There's the occasional, sensational,
drop-dead black dress of marvelous fabric, carved like a
sculpture, slit to infinity, that needs no accent except the

glorious expanse of skin it reveals. But, my darlings, for that LBD the body should be Christie Brinkley, the skin Isabella Rossellini, and the movements by Balanchine. Not for Everywoman.

So. We are Doing It with our clothes. We are vowing to never again wear a shroud of an LBD to even the most predictably boring party of the year. Even if we *don't* want to be noticed. Back in the Middle Ages almost everyone wore black—for the same reason—to fade into the background, to not call attention to themselves. But during those times Religion was of utmost importance in people's lives and they dressed, as you can see in portraits from the Middle Ages, almost identically to the way priests and nuns did. It is just amazing how often you walk into a party today where ninety percent of the guests look like novitiates in a religious order. The men in the ubiquitous Navy Blue Suit and the women in the Little Black Dress with, if any accent at all, a string of pearls from their high school graduation the size of baby teeth and worn just below the collarbone. If there's anything more unattractive than the LBD unadorned it has to be when it's accented with those little pearls. If you're really Doing It about yourself, you will either give them to your daughter for her prom dress or trade them in for some fakies of good quality, luster and size (approximately that of a large green grape) in both choker and matinee lengths. Never, ever, just below the collarbone!

Back to the Little Black Dress. (You probably realize by now that I feel as strongly about the LBD as I do about white wine. There are so many more delicious choices!) I am by no means saying that if you have a beautifully cut, classic black dress or suit and one gorgeous pin or the right size pearls it won't look terrific. It is just that you will blend in with ninety percent of the other women who are playing it safe, honestly believing they can't go wrong in a black dress that, uppermost in most of their minds, makes them look thinner. Granted, a dark color is slightly more slenderizing than a pale one but it is not enough to matter if you're Rubenesque. And speaking of Rubens, in all painting and sculpture black is known as negative space. And related as Art and Fashion are known to be and having spent a great part of my life involved in both fields, I offer this pearl of wisdom: Get out of that negative space! Get into flattering color and line. Why do you think the Impressionists are so universally appealing? It is their superb use of color that causes all of us to react so positively. To smile! To rejoice! To enjoy! As opposed to the negativity of the dark, the black. Can you think of any truly great painting of the Dutch School that, while admittedly dark, was not lighted effectively? Would Rembrandt's great soldier look half as good without his golden helmet? Or would Ver Meer's domestic scenes be quite as stunning without the glorious streaks of sunshine and light? And, moving along to the turn of the last century, certainly Sargent's magnificent *Madame X* in her sumptuous black velvet gown would not be as effective if that gown were not slit to a fare thee well exposing all that *crème fraîche* skin.

There are examples of how the color black is such a downer around us all the time that I can't emphasize it enough. But you must remember I mean unlighted, unaccented BLACK. A friend of mine in the fashion business, like so many women in that field, wears black day-in and night-out because it's easy, safe and, they foolishly think, "fashionable." A few weeks ago this lady appeared, as she's wont to do biannually, in a clear bright red, sheer-wool column of a dress with a choker of gold the only accent. She was her usual semi-annual smash. Why she doesn't retire some of her boring blacks and do this number with beige, silver grey, hot chocolate and more bright red, I will never know.

So if you're not decking all your blacks and other darks with LIGHT, you're not Doing It for yourself. Also, my darlings, you must learn about Color. I know there are color charts and books and clinics about color for your type. Your "type," according to these "experts," is determined by hair color, eyes, skin, etc., and in some cases, what kind of music, films, etc., you react to. Invariably, when I skim over one of these "tests" I find I'm not a "Summer," "Winter," "Spring," or "Fall" as they are so described but, rather, a mixture of all of them. As is Everyone Else. Sure, I like Beethoven, chocolate brown and skiing—which makes me a Winter. But I also love Sinatra, beige and peonies— which makes me a Spring. All of us are mixtures and you will be Doing It with color when you realize that.

The first thing to remember, or rather ignore, is all the old clichés about color. Redheads can't wear pink; olive skins should wear ultra-bright colors, and on and on. You can wear almost any color if the shade is right. That, to me, means that the color is usually "washed" with white as the Impressionists demonstrated with their true eye for beauty and perfection of color. Try to find a dark, murky turquoise or a mud red in any of their paintings. Never! But you can find an amazing number of murky, muddy colors on the racks and in the designers' showrooms. So to really be Doing It with color, you must discriminate. There are exceptions to every rule, but how many times in your life have you seen a really socko dress or suit in either deep

turquoise or fuchsia? I agree with the character in the book
Silk Lady by Gwen Davis who said he thought the color
fuchsia was outlawed as part of the Potsdam Treaty! Or
should have been!

Start Doing It Right with white or off-white or cream or
vanilla. Remember what the Impressionists did with
white/light, and some of the legendary film stars, like Merle
Oberon, who refused to wear any other color and furnished
every one of her homes in the same shade. That's knowing
the impact, the flattery of one color. Imagine, if you will,
Merle O. decked out in one of her white outfits—whether
a blazer and slacks or a ball gown. Imagine if, with the blazer,
she had a deep marine blue (another color that should have
been outlawed in the Potsdam Treaty) scarf and red shoes
and purse which most saleswomen, even in the designer
section of a boutique or department store, would recommend. Ordinary. Predictable. Then imagine the same
blazer suit with white shoes, purse and maybe a black tiny-
dotted white scarf. Smashing! And that's the way old Merle
did it and will always be remembered as a vision in white—
undisturbed by blobs of distracting, unrelated colors. Not
to say we recommend you drifting around your office,
supermarket and daily rounds in white—a bit impractical
when you are not transported by an immaculate limo. The
point is you are Doing It for yourself when you realize the
colors that are most flattering to you and emphasize those
colors. Learning the flatterers is very simple. With good
lighting to start, hold up to your face a sweater, scarf, blouse,
dress or robe in every shade from white, pale pink, pale
beige or grey to the brightest reds, oranges and rusts to the
darkest bottle greens, chocolate browns and, yes, even the
ubiquitous black. (There are a handful of women, all under

thirty, who *can* wear high necked blacks, unadorned, but even they must have the crème fraîche skin of Sargent's *Madame X* to get away with it.) Be honest with yourself. Do It. Forget the "in" color of the year—unless it's *flattering to you.*

It is almost ironic that in the middle of writing about how you are Not Doing It for yourself if you're shrouded in black most of the time, we went to the world premiere of Menotti's opera *Goya.* There, on stage at the Kennedy Center, the glorious vocalist Victoria Vergara, as the Duchess of Alba, was breathtaking not only in her singing but in her appearance in the first two acts. Never having seen her before, I had heard about the exquisite voice but was not prepared for the matching looks. Stunning! Now in both the scenes she was wearing either pale yellow or a luscious creme color that emphasized her dark hair and equally creamy skin. *Alors!* In the third act, I couldn't believe it was the same woman. She looked completely different—hard and coarse and there was no change of hair or makeup (we were sitting very close) or any supposed advance in time. But she was wearing black—unadorned—and was a glowing example of how to go from a stunner to a drabber in one act! When she was dying in a later act, she wore a creamy color and looked her exquisite self.

It is always a real downer when the fall clothes arrive in the shops. The parade of what I call the mud colors—flattering to no one on earth—commences. Those deep, blackened purples, what is called "winter navy" (the worst!), soured wines and dried dark browns. Occasionally a clear, bright "up" red saves the day. Again—it is the *tone*—the way the color is mixed that makes the difference. Compare the exquisite violets of Velázquez (and Monet, Degas, etc.) with the inky purples you see so often in the stores. If you are Doing It with color, you will soon develop an eye for the right tone and be able to seek out the tone or shade that does it for you whether it is a lovely violet, a soft wine or a warm russet. The right colors are there—but you have to really seek them out; recognize the ones which flatter you, which is part of Doing It for yourself.

CHAPTER IV

THE EYES HAVE IT
(Only If You Use Them!)

It never ceases to amaze me that often people can see a work of art (or another person or object) and each one sees something other than just the façade. Then again, others never go beyond the facade. That is why we must learn to use our eyes by observing: recognizing and recording in that expandable file called our brain. What works and what doesn't in life is the key to Doing It for yourself. Some of our greatest artists never took a drawing lesson but there isn't one great one who hasn't studied the techniques of the masters to see what made them work. Picasso and Braque "borrowed" ideas from one another. Picasso was "inspired" by his great rival Matisse, especially Matisse's *La Danse.* Matisse owed a debt to Chardin and Monet. The list goes on and on. Even in fashion, the greatest influence of the twentieth century, Chanel, never took a sewing lesson. And she grew up in the small French town of Moulins, which was not exactly the sixteenth arrondissement of Paris. But she was Doing It with her eyes. She *digested* the fashion magazines—not just flipped through. She soon realized why the featured fashions worked—why they were right. She also observed the fashionable ladies of her hometown and again zeroed in on just why they always looked magnifique. O.K., so a beau set her up with her own hat shop for starters (as did many other monsieurs during her lifetime), but without that innate taste, that pure sense of style, her Observing and Recording, we would never have the legend that is Chanel. If you were not born with an educated or developed eye—and most of us were not—the only way to achieve one is through observation and exposure. Joseph Hirshhorn, founder of the Hirshhorn Museum and Sculpture Garden in Washington, D.C., was a poor, immigrant boy who would study for hours at a time the advertising calendars which featured photographs of famous paintings. This endeavor led him into museums to seek out the originals. By the time he was in his late teens, his eye was so developed, as well as his talent for making money, he was able to buy a small masterpiece with the first money he made trading on the "curb" exchange on Wall Street. The point being that Joseph Hirshhorn was Doing It with his eye from childhood and, through his lifetime, made very few mistakes. Of course, when you collect almost twelve thousand paintings and sculptures every one of them can't be a Masterpiece of the First Order. There aren't that many in the entire world. However, studying those calendars and going to museums when he wasn't working at odd jobs paved the way for an extraordinary collection of which we are all the beneficiaries. The stories about this amazing and colorful man are legion. Dominant among them are, of course, that famous "eye" and how he loved to bargain. One of the favorite eye stories was in the early forties when he was starting to form his collection. He happened into the studio of Willem de Kooning in New York. De Kooning, one of the early Abstract Expressionists, was just beginning to make waves among the art *cognesi*. Hirshhorn took a long look at the bold, abstract and semi-abstract works hanging from nails on the walls or leaning against one another on the floor. The colors were overwhelmingly beautiful; the figures—when there were suggestions of figures—were slashed, distorted and the most imaginative Joseph Hirshhorn had ever seen.

"I'll take them!" Hirshhorn said to de Kooning.

"Them?" said the gentle artist. "Which ones?"

"Every single one of them!" replied Hirshhorn, reaching for his checkbook and thereby launching himself as a major collector, while giving the young de Kooning the first big boost in his now legendary career.

If he had not been Doing It Right with his eye—observing, absorbing, digesting, inhaling everything in order to know what separates the mediocre from the great—Joe Hirshhorn would never have been able to make a decision like that, or any of the countless others that made his collection so great.

Many are the tales about his bargaining—even with Picasso. Picasso, being almost as astute about business as he was about his art, loved the little American who would drive the hardest of bargains while enjoying the hospitality of Picasso's villa. Drinking Picasso's wine and eating his exquisite meals, Hirshhorn would still wage war about the price.

My favorite of Hirshhorn's "bargaining" stories is a personal one. As I mentioned before, I am a docent at the Hirshhorn Museum and Sculpture Garden here in Washington, D.C., and there I fell in love with one of the museum's acquisitions in the late seventies. It is an architectural painting of an old building in Soho (N.Y.) done in Photo-Realist style—only with a difference. The artist, H. N. Han, uses an air gun and hundreds of stencils and the result is a realistic version of the building with a hazy finish that is achieved by spraying thousands of color dots, much like Seurat, on the surface. Hard to describe but equally hard not to find enchanting. It is so exquisitely beautiful we always have a small mob scene around it at the museum. I couldn't stand not having a Han of our very own so my husband and I went to his dealer in New York, decided on Han's breathtaking view of the New York skyline in Impressionist colors and had it shipped to Washington, where it is in commanding view of our center hall. We had a little party for the unveiling of the masterpiece, attended by the Hirshhorns. He kept circling around it and finally said, "Can I ask you what you paid for it, Dorothy? I know Han's dealer and he's tough."

"Oh, sure you can," I replied. "I know he's a tough one, Mr. Hirshhorn, but I'm like you. I know how to bargain and I really got him to knock the price down quite a bit."

"O.K.," said Hirshhorn. "What did you pay for it?"

Proudly, I told him the amount we paid for the painting. Hirshhorn's face glowed. He smiled and shook his head. "Nah, he still got you, kid!"

Hirshhorn used the term "kid" affectionately and indiscriminately. One time I asked him if he knew my father, who also had worked on Wall Street for many years, and was still doing so. "What's his name?" asked Hirshhorn. I told him. "Oh, yeah," he said. "Give the kid my best!" The "kid" in this case being only a few years younger than Himself.

But back to that important Eye. To be Doing It Right with your eye, you have to educate it; you have to observe constantly, whether it is in art, fashion, decorating or any other field. Like Joseph Hirshhorn, I have been fascinated by pictures since I was a little girl. Growing up in New York—exposed to all the greats in the Met, the Whitney and MOMA—certainly helped develop the eye. Then, as a teenager, spending several hours a week in the Museum of Modern Art between fashion shots and returning to the same fascinating paintings and sculptures that at first seemed distorted, my eye became used to different artists reacting in their own specific way to what ordinary mortals see only one way, the way a camera would capture it. By continual exposure and observation, my eye became so accustomed to the unusual, unpredictable, challenging colors and shapes of contemporary art that eventually the traditional became too dull, too ordinary, too predictable. But that conclusion took many years of Doing It with the eye. One thing is sure—you will never learn to appreciate fine art if you visit a museum or gallery only occasionally. You must go back; be that interested, that challenged, to go back again and again. All the experts can't be wrong. Great works of art are not in museums because just one or two people like them. All the experts concur on every painting and sculpture you see. Unlike the days when the Impressionists were rejected because two or three people in charge refused change, every piece donated or bought must pass several boards and committees before it is even considered.

And that is not to say the public must love every piece. They usually fight change too, and still tend to believe that art must be a landscape, portrait or still life. (And hundreds of years ago, religious paintings were all they would accept.)

It is the same with music. If all you listen to is pop and never give classical music a chance, you will never enjoy one of the greatest treasures we have. And you can't "get it" in one sitting, either. You must be willing to pry open your mind.

I am always amused when someone I meet will say, "Oh, I know you work at the Hirshhorn, and I paint (usually on Sunday) and I'd like to have some of my art in the museum." No fooling! Well, I paint too and I know that even with the sharpest dealer/agent in the world (unfortunately, that's sometimes how it's done), my work could never hang along with the giants—and never should. To be part of a major museum's collection is undoubtedly the goal of every artist. But that doesn't mean that if you do paint—daily or even only on Sundays, or are taking classes in drawing or painting—that you shouldn't have goals. Getting your work into community art shows is the first step. Then, as you improve—into local galleries and who knows after that? At least, you're Doing It. And along the way, you are, of course, using your EYE to observe, observe; absorb, absorb what makes every fine painting or sculpture work—in every gallery or museum you visit, when you're not putting your brush to the canvas. Because you will learn more about good painting in the museums than you ever will in an art class. But we take the classes because most of us need the technical knowledge we learn in the classroom in order to know how to mix the paints, prepare the canvas, and so on.

So, if you are Doing It with oils, watercolors or clay, you can sometimes skip a class, but don't ever give up using your Eye in the galleries and museums. Shows change about every six weeks and there's always something new, controversial and stimulating to see and absorb. Even if you are not painting or sculpting and are simply Doing It with

Art—going to lectures and seminars, even going back to college or just starting with noncredit art history courses— Doing the museums and galleries with a passion (I promise you—you will, once you're hooked)—it will be the most rewarding step you ever took in your lifetime. Certainly the dividends of learning (and loving) art and its history, which stay with you forever, are far more rewarding than losing a few inches or meeting a new man or going on a trip. We all do those things at some point. But Art is something that is joyously, intellectually with you through all your inches on or off; through every new man, and every single trip. In fact, it gives traveling a completely new dimension when you know that in almost every city, in every country in the world, there is a great work or works of art to see, absorb, record and, most of all, Enjoy! Like Vincent Price says, *"Art is everywhere and where it isn't, I don't want to go."*

So start developing your Eye. Let it work to your advantage. Whatever you see—absorb, record. Whether it is a room photographed in a magazine, a work of art or someone's knockout outfit—Do It with your EYE. Let your eye photograph and record the room. Figure out why it is appealing. Is it the colors—the overall design—the accessories? Is it a combination of all three factors? Most likely it is—but if you only look at the picture and don't absorb it—you will never be able to figure why certain things work. The same rules apply to art and fashion. The overall design (composition in art), color and accessories are the Big Three. There isn't a masterpiece in the world that isn't beautifully composed with memorable colors and a frame (accessory) that compliments it. In Art, however, the frame will never make or break a painting. If it is wrong, it can take away from the picture, but it is the easiest thing in the world to change. As in fashion, the accessories will never make the design of a dress or suit work, but if they are wrong, they can just about ruin it.

In decorating, there are many more "accessories" to consider. I remember a group discussing an exceptionally beautiful room in a house on a tour for a charity here in Washington. All of the following statements were made:

"It's the art—the combination of styles—and how they were put together."

"No, it's the colors—the way the colors of the art and furnishings are related."

"It is the lighting that does it. Lighting is never considered that important—but this room proves how much it matters. Every lamp, every painting light is perfectly placed. If you moved one of them, the effect would not be as stunning."

And on and on. The owner and/or decorator of the house was obviously Doing It Right with her eye. Everything worked. And yet there are many rooms and many homes that are decorated by professionals where everything seems to work but there's something wrong. If you have become proficient at Doing It with your Eye, you will pick it up immediately. No matter how people rave over a seemingly perfect, or let's settle for "beautiful" room or home, if you have developed your eye you will be able to detect immediately the reason it sometimes is not. It's too glitzy, too overdone, too "matched," too "decorated." Sometimes it is the absence of books, magazines, plants or flowers—or too many of the very same things. If you have really learned to Do It with your Eye, you have really learned to edit, to add and subtract. And the very room or home that needs it may be your own.

Remember here what Madeleine Castaing, who for many connoisseurs was the Mme. Grès of French decor, said, "I can go into a house and tell you the social standing of the person who lives there; his degree of culture and who his friends are."

So get to work. Observe. Absorb. Record. Start Doing It with your Eye. It is something you can do, enjoy and become proficient at for the rest of your life.

CHAPTER V

THE WAY THEY WERE

We all have aspirations, dreams and fantasies. Most of us don't act on them and they remain just that—fantasies. Why? Because we are lazy.

Speaking of lazy—the easy way out—always makes me think of so many Americans I know who were living in Europe, as I was, in Germany, very close to Munich. A good many of them never traveled, even though Paris was half a day away, ate most of their meals at home or in the Officers' Club, and complained all the time about small inconsequential inconveniences. They all had maids, cooks and hausmeisters, as we did, and absolutely beautiful surroundings. Instead of Doing It—traveling and experiencing the history and culture of Europe (Everything So Close and So Great)—many of them pined away for Podunk, USA, and did nothing but go to American movies and wax longingly about the wonders of McDonald's. These are the same kind of people who live in the suburbs of New York or Washington and go into the city once a year. They never take advantage of theaters, museums, or any of the great treasures the cities offer. And this went on even before the cities became overcrowded and troubled.

Even though I was twenty-three years old at the time and had never joined a club in my life before (or since), I became president of the German-American Women's Association, made up mainly of artists and writers and some of the finest women I have ever known. I still shed *eine kleine* tear every time I look at the beautiful sculpted tray made for me by one of my German friends and signed by all of them. The artist who created the tray, incidentally, was crippled by a bombing in World War II. And there she is, Paula, my German friend, maimed so badly she can hardly stand but she is still Doing It and that is our point. It's only human to take the easy way. It is easier, isn't it, to watch television than to practice music, write a résumé, draw that bowl of roses or just go out and take a brisk walk. It's easier, too, to brush our goals aside and say, "I'm really not good enough to reach the top"; "I can't act, draw, dance (or whatever) well enough"; "I didn't go to Yale or Harvard or wherever." We have said them all; we have heard them all. Excuses. They are just not good enough! Not in this country where none of that matters. You do need Confidence and Determination, which are almost more important than talent, education, looks or anything else. Of course, we must have a modicum of talent, education and input along with large dollops of Confidence and Determination.

Two favorite stories of people who Did It and are still Doing It are those of actor Richard Dreyfuss and lawyer-writer-editor Steven Brill.

When Dreyfuss was nine years old and the family had moved from New York to California, he announced to his mother that he wanted to be an actor. "Don't just talk about it. Do something about it. *Now,*" she said. Dreyfuss got up and walked down to the Community Center Theatre and started working at it that very afternoon. That has got to be my favorite Doing It story. Kudos and Oscars came later.

The other inspiring, just plain Doing It folktale is that of Steven Brill, who grew up in Queens, New York, the son of a liquor store owner. While he was recovering from a basketball injury that shattered his kneecap in 1964 when he was in junior high school, he was reading a biography of John F. Kennedy (and not, you'll notice, watching TV or playing games). He asked his mother, "What's Choate?" She told him it was a prep school, like a college, except that you attend it in your high school years.

"You mean it has all those buildings and hockey rinks and swimming pools and you're not even in college yet," asked Steven, who immediately wrote away for a guide to prep schools. He rejected Choate because it had no swimming pool and ended up in Deerfield Academy in Massachusetts. Of course, it helped that young Brill's junior high school average was 99.9. He was Doing It in a big way even as a young teenager. Notice, too, he was playing basketball when he broke his kneecap, not "hanging out," that term for doing nothing. So he was more than one-dimensional even then.

The headmaster at Deerfield was so impressed with Steven he offered him a scholarship that allowed his parents to pay only what they could afford. From Deerfield he went to Yale (an article he wrote while there appeared on the op-ed page of the *New York Times*) and graduated summa cum laude, Phi Beta Kappa. Steven then went to the Yale Law School and, while there, was already Doing It, working for John Lindsay and writing for *New York* magazine, where he went to work after graduating in 1975. In 1977, he researched and wrote a best-selling book on a topic that had frustrated many more experienced writers, the Teamsters Union. A few years later, Brill founded and edited *American Lawyer* magazine. He now has a legal news empire and conducts management seminars for lawyers at $1,000 for a two-day session. In covering at length many merger-and-acquisition lawyers, Steven became an expert deal-maker himself. Despite all his business acumen and the activity and hard work that goes into his Am-Law newspapers, Steven says that "psychologically, I only feel I'm working when I'm writing articles. The rest is pure fun." If he hasn't written anything in a week (only lectured, made crucial decisions, masterminded legal deals), Brill feels he hasn't DONE anything. Doing It, for Steven Brill, obviously means Doing many things and Doing them consistently well.

We can't all be Brills or, lest the feminists howl, Clare Boothe Luce (from caption writer for *Vogue* to playwright to Congresswoman to Ambassador), or Sherry Lansing (former head of a major motion picture studio), or the irrepressible Sherrye Henry of Memphis, Tennessee, who, eighteen years ago with no experience at all, talked a New York City radio station into allowing her to work free. In exchange for a desk and typewriter, she agreed to produce and broadcast stories for the air, which, if accepted, would earn the current AFTRA rate—$5.25. The first week she took home $26.25. Six weeks later she was hired for the news staff. Today she has the most popular interview program in the city.

Obviously there are thousands of success stories in our land of opportunity (yes, even today), but that is not our primary concern. It is the END of our goal. Our primary goal is the initial action of DOING IT RIGHT. Making that phone call; writing that letter (like Brill, for brochures that changed his life); flopping on the floor and DOING your exercises; starting your diet at the very next meal; enrolling in the course or courses TODAY that will change and enrich your life forever.

And all of you out there who want to meet new people— go ahead—join that health club or church group. Become a "friend" to your local museum. *Read* the newspapers. In every paper—almost every day—there are notices to join in local theater, art, garden, animal, sports and literary groups.

But you have got to Do It! And Doing It Right, I am sure you have learned by now, entails Observing. Observing how the people you admire, for whatever reason, Do It. They very seldom talk about it, but if you ask, yes, they do exercise; they have read the articles or books being discussed; they have seen the controversial art exhibit; they wrote to the editor about something that moved them; they chased a dream or two. In other words, they Do It! And I'm sure you've noticed that nine out of ten times the people who go to the fat farms a couple of times a year never change in size or shape. Oh, they may come home a few pounds lighter but immediately put the weight back on because they don't believe they can Do It themselves, or rather want someone to do it for them. Instead, by spending a lot of money, this "miracle" of losing weight is going to happen to them. Even if it's only a few pounds that they lose they think they can eat like porkies and then go back for the "miracle" again. That, of course, is letting someone else Do It for you, which, of course, does not count or achieve honest results.

So, all you would-be Doers, get down on the floor right now and FEEL those hips and thighs trim down. It not only

Feels good down there and wherever else you whittle down but up where it counts even more—that part of your brain that dispenses how you FEEL about yourself. Believe me, darlings, your self esteem will be a million times higher than if you pay someone to try to pound the flesh off.

And, please, don't use that horrendous expression when people ask if you have read a particular story in the paper, "Oh, I never read newspapers; they're too depressing!" Anyone who uses that line is a blithering idiot. As long as there are two people alive in this world, we will have disagreements, controversy and lots of other negatives. But once you get past the front-page stories, you'll find all the good things that are going on in our world, that are there for you to take, enjoy, change and feast upon. Again, *mein Herz*, let me quote from *Auntie Mame:* "The world is a banquet just there for the taking. But most poor suckers don't even go to the table for a nibble!" Start nibbling. Start partaking. Start digesting Everything you see and hear. Start Doing It!

And, under the heading of "The Way They Were," how can I ever forget my meeting with Bobby Kennedy in Leningrad? . . .

My then-husband and I were on our way to Moscow for a two-year diplomatic tour of duty at the American Embassy, where my spouse was an army attaché. We had stayed in London for two months of briefing and then we were assigned to take the luxury liner *Batory* to Leningrad, where we were to be met by two American officers from the Embassy, who would escort us into Moscow. Being four months pregnant at the time, with a one-year-old and a three-year-old in tow, it was not the easiest trip I have ever undertaken—although I did find that traveling with a diplomatic passport gave one a status above first class. No matter the ship, airline or train, you had the choice compartments, you were the first to be served—and the first on or off. On a ship, you dined at the Captain's Table if that was your choice. So it was certainly not the accommodations that left me queasy. More likely it was the fact that traveling by ship from New York to London, then London to Leningrad would leave me seasick even today. I remember that I have never had a desire to kiss the ground before or since; but debarking the *Batory* in Leningrad as we marched down the red- carpeted gangway, I really had to restrain myself from doing so.

That trip from London to Leningrad was not without a prologue of intrigue. We were joined by another diplomatic couple also en route to Moscow, to the British Embassy: the Senior Military Attaché, Brigadier and Mrs. Davidson-Houston. The Brigadier, his uniform covered by ribbons from World War II, and his lovely wife became like substitute parents to us during our trip and throughout our stay in Moscow. This despite the fact that Missy, our one-year-old, would lob a bit of food over to the Brigadier at almost every meal, then proceed to bang her spoon on her high-chair with glee when she hit her target. We were horrified. But the Davidson-Houstons had grandchildren in England whom they already missed, so they just beamed at the activity. But then too, they were diplomats!

After dinner in the luxurious dining salon of the *Batory* every evening, where the Captain joined us once or twice, we would saunter down to the cafe. The children were put to sleep, watched over by a nanny, and the Davidson-Houstons would also retire. The cafe would be roaring with music, dancing and heated conversations. The first night out, we were joined by Georgians, who, like most natives of that region refer to themselves as Georgians rather than Russians. They are a warm, hearty, happy people—perhaps because they live in the south of that enormous country, where winters are less severe. The group we partied with were all young, in their twenties as we were, and were fascinated with America. They knew more about our music, theater and books than many Americans do. So we talked, we danced—Georgian and American style; we drank the wonderful Georgian wines of which they are so justly proud; and we had one of the most memorable evenings of our lives. Early the next morning, six bottles of that glorious Georgian wine were delivered to our stateroom with a lovely note signed: *Nicolai, Vladimir, Yuri, Aleki and Sasha.* We never saw them again! We skirted the ship by day and went to the cafe every night for the rest of the trip, but no one seemed to know whom we were talking about. It was an early lesson in all we had been taught about the intrigue and the devious ways of the Soviet state. It was *our* fault, really. We should have known better than to become that friendly with Soviet citizens. It obviously made it too difficult for them. Nicolai, Vlad, Yuri, Aleki and Sasha—wherever you are—I think of you often as the fabulous five, the good guys of the U.S.S.R. I know there are millions like you and you will always be symbols of how wonderful your countrymen really are.

We were met in Leningrad by Major Kevin Fitzpatrick and Captain Richard Lawrence of the American Embassy Staff in Moscow, and escorted to the Astoria Hotel, but not before I was completely overwhelmed by the enchanting beauty of the "northern capital." Small wonder it was called the "Window on the West" when it was known as St. Petersburg. It is the only city in the Soviet Union with a decidedly European flavor. Many of its architectural triumphs were built by French or Italian artisans, including, of course, the magnificent Hermitage and Winter Palace. The Astoria Hotel, our residence for a few days before moving on to Moscow, was also a Baroque palace of gigantic public rooms, marble stairways and chandeliers that vied with those of Versailles. It is truly one of the most beautiful palaces in the world.

Our suites were equally luxurious: two damask-swathed bedrooms separated by a stunning silk and satin sitting room. Antique French furniture filled the three rooms. Even the baby's bed was an exceptionally beautiful flower-bedecked antique crib, already in place—not so incidentally. Soviet Intelligence is beyond excellent, even down to the ages of the diplomatic children residing in their country! In each room, the focal point opposite each fireplace was a curio cabinet of lacquered wood, edged in gold and filled with objets d'art: jeweled eggs, china and decorative dolls in old Russian military uniforms and costumes. I'm sure the eggs were not Fabergé or I would have been tempted to hoist a few and been declared persona non grata right off!

After a few days of Hermitaging, attending the Kirov Ballet and being overwhelmed at the stunning architecture of Leningrad and its Impressionistic colors, it was on to Moscow.

We had heard from our Consul in Leningrad that Robert Kennedy was making a tour of the U.S.S.R. with Supreme Court Justice William O. Douglas, and they were staying at the Astoria Hotel. We did not run into them, however, until our last day there. Talk about Doing It Right. This was it!

We were descending the gigantic marble staircase from our second-floor rooms on the morning of our departure for Moscow, with the children, the officers from the Embassy and the Consul General, when I saw Kennedy and Justice Douglas at the reception desk at the foot of the sweeping, curved staircase.

Suddenly, there was an explosion of Soviets surrounding us—the heretofore kindly old concierge on our floor leading the pack of men and women screaming and yelling, *"Vor, vor, grabital!"* ("Thief, thief, robber!") The little person they surrounded and scared to death was Cynthia, our three-year-old. Clutched in her hand was one of the little Russian dolls from the curio cabinet in her bedroom. She literally froze on the steps as the Russians surrounded her. Bobby Kennedy dropped his bags, ran up the steps and gathered her in his arms. We all looked on, shocked and horrified at the fuss they made over the incident, so obviously an innocent one. Cynthia said later that the cabinet was like the shelves of dolls she had at home and she only wanted to add a Russian doll "to play with the other ones."

But for those immediate moments—which seemed eternal—confusion reigned, and only Kennedy's sharp reprimands to the accusing staff and his gentle, soothing words to Cynthia had any effect. The Consul and the other officers, including my husband, could not calm the Soviets. Somehow that strident, high-pitched Boston-accented voice in a combination of English and Russian brought them to a halt. He demanded to know how they could scare a little girl like that, when all they had to do was to inform us and calmly request the doll's return. The Kennedy authority and forcefulness worked wonders, and the fact that he and Justice Douglas were surrounded by high-ranking Soviets didn't hurt either. They, too, had cast several heavy frowns and vociferous *"nyets"* on the happening. As I recovered Cynthia from the strong Kennedy arms, I thanked Bobby

and told him he probably prevented an international incident, that the Soviets would call "The Doll Caper." He
laughed and said knowingly that many American diplomats
had been "P and Gee'd" (declared persona non grata) for
less. How right he was!

While we all had coffee and chocolate in the Astoria
dining room, Bobby told me that his sisters, Patricia Kennedy Lawford, Jean Kennedy Smith and Eunice Kennedy
Shriver, were also touring the Soviet Union and would be in
Moscow the week after we arrived. Coincidentally, one of
our escorts, Major Fitzpatrick, also of Boston origins, was
related to the Kennedy clan. His wife, Helen, was hosting a
tea the next week to welcome me to the Embassy and to
honor the visiting Kennedy sisters. What I particularly
remember about that tea was Patricia Kennedy Lawford
passing around pictures and the baby (the youngest at the
time) being held by his father, Peter Lawford, the actor.
This was in the very late fifties, when Lawford was in his
prime, and the response around the room was unanimous:
"Mmm, he is darling! Ah, is he cute!" And no one meant
the baby.

Speaking of Helen Fitzpatrick, the hostess of that particular tea, she hosted another rather memorable event at
their quarters in the Embassy soon after, when Billy Rose
and his wife, Joyce, were visiting. While Helen's husband,
Fitz, was distantly related to the Kennedy clan, Helen was
the daughter of Polish parents, who spoke their native
tongue almost exclusively. Hence, Helen was quite proficient in Russian, which is similar. And even though many
of us at the Embassy knew this, she would tell many of the
other foreign diplomats who complimented her on her
language skills that she studied Russian at Columbia Univer-

sity, and that along with her husband and other army attachés she had received a master's degree.

I won't go into Helen's other idiosyncrasies, which eventually became an embarrassment to the Embassy as well as to other Americans there. She was living proof of Doing It All ·Wrong. Because of Helen's behavior, the Fitzpatricks were almost P and Gee'd a number of times. The fact that Fitz himself was one of the most valuable members of the diplomatic staff (and a living saint, to boot) kept that from happening. Our Russian chauffeurs would tell us that Major Fitzpatrick was the only American at the Embassy whose Russian was absolutely perfect. Everyone else had some sort of accent.

But back to the dinner party Helen was giving for Billy Rose and his wife. Now, all the diplomatic wives—State Department, Army, Navy and Marines—had been drilled here in the States about the protocol, rank and seating of these dinners and had been furnished with extensive china, crystal and silver if they did not care to bring their own. Most of the dinner parties we had were for one purpose: to achieve better relations with our allies as well as our not-so-allied. And most of these dinners had a mixture of foreign diplomats and a smattering of other Americans. As I mentioned in the diet and exercise section of the book, the meals consisted of several courses and several wines. These were served by our Russian maids, and if it was a particularly large dinner party we would borrow maids from other Embassy officers, because if you were not giving a dinner party on a specific night, you were attending one. It was almost always black tie or full-dress uniform and formal gowns for the women.

The maids, many of whom had worked at the Embassy for years (and also, I must add, for the KGB), wore the standard evening uniform of black with white cuffs, apron and cap. We had to order several of these uniforms through catalogues from the States, and I guess some of the maids who had worked at the Embassy for fifteen or twenty years must have had extensive collections. The uniforms brought a very good price on the black market. In this case, it was usually the basic "big" black dress.

Where Ruth had run into Billy Rose and his wife, I have no idea. There had been no official reception for him by our Ambassador. But I would guess it was at the Bolshoi Theater. Most tourists attend at least one performance of the ballet at that spectacular theater. The first ten or twelve rows are always roped off in velvet for diplomatic use only, and most of us took advantage of that perk quite often. Many times, we would be approached at intermissions by American tourists curious about our diplomatic life in Moscow. One time at the Bolshoi, I met Jack Kriedler of the "21 Club" in New York and I told him how my parents had loved the club and how now it was my very own favorite. He beamed and said he would love to trade an evening at the "21" for an evening at the Embassy! "Done," I told him as we were honoring the Brits a few nights later. I included Mr. K, and I'm still enjoying evenings at the "21," even though both Kriedlers are no longer there.

So, I assume Helen met the Billy Roses at the Bolshoi, and when she asked me to attend the party I accepted—I was very curious to hear about the marvelous Rose art collection. There were no formal written invitations, as is usual for official dinner parties, but it was black tie and Helen had roped in the Dutch Ambassador and his wife, the

French Naval Attaché, the Egyptian Military Attaché, two Italian journalists and a handful of Americans. I had not been in the Fitzpatricks' apartment since the Kennedy tea, but I remembered I tripped over a lone tricycle wheel as I entered and was caught by a tiny little man who turned out to be Billy Rose.

"My wife did the same thing," he said, laughing, "only you did it better." His wife, Joyce, an ex-showgirl and absolutely gorgeous, showed me where she tore her gown as she made *her* trip over the wheel.

Balled-up papers were lying about on the carpet and chairs, and toys were scattered all over; there was even a jar of baby food on a side table. I was mortified that a fellow American, especially on diplomatic duty, could live this way. The other Americans there were all trying to shove things under the rug with their feet or under a pillow if one was close by. I can still see the Dutch Ambassador's wife trying to put her drink down on a table while pushing the baby-food jar gently aside.

Billy and Joyce Rose were in very high spirits and did not seem to care, and we had an animated conversation about his art collection. I also remarked on how unusual Joyce's pearls were. "Oh, honey, these are the new pop-its," she said; and she did just that—popped them and they came apart. "I have real ones at home, this size, can you imagine? But Billy didn't want me to travel with them. So these looked the closest to the realies. Aren't they great?" They were, and she sent them to me the next day because she said I would never be able to find anything like them in the Soviet Union. She had tried to do some serious shopping in Moscow and came up with nothing.

As we finally sat down at the dinner table, there was a
decided hush as Helen's maid, Tanya, shuffled into the
room with the first of many platters of food. No uniform
covered Tanya but, rather, what a previous generation would
have called a "housedress"; "multi-fleured" would be a nice
way of saying that thousands of flowers were growing with
abandon all over the food-stained surface. On her head was
a torn nylon stocking stretched to its limit by Tanya's bul-
bous head. And the shuffling of feet! I peeked down as she
waddled by and caught sight of the felt carpet slippers whose
backs were crushed down by her hefty heels. To top it all
off, as she served each person Tanya would yell, *"Cushit,
cushit!"* ("Eat, eat!") There were many people who almost
choked that night, Billy Rose among them.

Helen's way of Doing It was obviously all wrong and is a
typical example of no matter how many times certain people
are exposed to Doing It Right, no matter how often they are
told, it still has no effect. It continues to come up wrong.
It is like a garden of carefully tended plants, all fed, fertilized
and tenderly cared for. One or two will wither away or never
really surface. I guess that is nature, human or otherwise.

To go to the other extreme, that of Doing It Right, with
taste, style and in this case that lovely word "glory," we can't
leave the Diplomatic Colony without meeting Stan Turner.

I had heard about this brave, glorious Canadian hero who
had run off as a boy of seventeen to join the squadron of
super-daring R.A.F. pilots trained by the famous Douglas
Bader. Bader, an Englishman, had lost both legs after being
shot down by the Germans early in World War II. Instead of
retiring after receiving two artificial limbs, he climbed back
into the cockpit and taught squadrons of young Canadians
and Brits how to fly daringly and brilliantly. Stan Turner

was one of these great pilots trained by Douglas Bader, and he returned to Canada after the war as that nation's most honored, decorated war hero.

Stan had married his beautiful wife, Mary Ann, before she was out of her teens, and of course she accompanied him to Moscow when he was dispatched for duty as Canada's chief air attaché. I met Mary Ann, who taught art at the British-American Diplomatic School, and at a Belgian reception soon after we arrived I looked forward to meeting the formidable Stan. There was Mary Ann, standing with a Canadian officer whose chest was covered with ribbons and whose shoulder was circled with the thick gold aiguillette that identified the military attaché. Except that this one was right out of Central Casting! Early Tom Selleck would be the most accurate description. "This must be the fabled Stan," I ventured.

"No, actually this is Ken Campbell, our colleague," Mary Ann said. "Here's Stan, over here!" She guided me across to another group. Smiling and extending both hands to me was the affable, warm and benign-looking man who was one of the greatest heroes of World War II. Reckless, daring and intrepid were the words used to describe him in action. But sweet, soft and kind suited him much more (when he was not shooting down Nazi planes). Doing It gloriously—when it really counted—that was Stan Turner. And the following year, when the British movie *Reach For the Sky* was released, a large group of us went over to the British Embassy to see it and cheer. Cheer, we did. But both Stan and Mary Ann were a bit embarrassed at the casting of rather tough young thug types as Stan and his fellow flyers. They may have been wild young men, but they certainly weren't future gangsters (as Stan said). I read Douglas Bader's book, from which the movie was made, and it was truly inspirational—as were Stan and his fellow airmen. It was Doing It of the First Order.

There are so many stories from those diplomatic days in Moscow . . . the fabulous Peter Rawls, one of the British naval attachés, whose great-uncle was British Ambassador at the turn of the century, and whose scarlet-lined cloak young Peter wore, flourishing it for the crowds who used to gather to see us—crowds dressed to the hilt, arriving and departing Embassy parties . . . the time the Shah of Iran and his wife visited and the big flap about whether the Americans should curtsy when presented (we didn't) . . . the time the great ballerina Mia Plisetskaya danced solo for the diplomatic children at their holiday party at the Kremlin . . . and how I was chatting away with a charming Belgian at a huge reception a few nights after our arrival in Moscow, admiring the Croix de Guerre in his lapel and receiving a special invitation to a spectacular dinner dance at the Belgian Embassy—finding out that I'd been chatting (earlier) with the Ambassador himself! (The Belgians had flown in thousands of fresh flowers for that one, and it was spectacular.)

Everyone—well, almost everyone—was Doing It well in those heady years in Moscow, but that's another book, my darlings. So I'll get on with this one now.

As a last and rather bittersweet anecdote of those years in Moscow, there was the Greatest Example of Doing It Right—that was actually a matter of life and death.

You'll remember that I mentioned I was *enceinte* when we arrived in Moscow. We had an American Air Force doctor in our Embassy and there was a British M.D. in the British. For anything serious you were advised to go to the American Hospital in West Berlin. For the wives who were pregnant, this was a must. We had all heard horror stories of a couple of women who had either waited too long or who had an early delivery, and how in the Soviet hospital's labor room—with no assistance or help from medical personnel—women were writhing and screaming in a manner reminiscent of scenes in *The Snake Pit*. However, I was fine throughout, and early in my eighth month took off for Berlin.

Driving to the Moscow airport that early-February evening, with snow coming down in golf-ball size, the chauffeur had to stop several times to shovel it off the windshield. No matter, the Soviet planes take off in ANYTHING. Although the flight was extremely rough, I was busy caring for my two little daughters and for once didn't have time to be motion-sick myself. When we landed in Warsaw, midway between Moscow and Berlin, the runway was so slick with ice that we skidded into the tail of another plane. Then finally we arrived at the airport in East Berlin, where a staff car was waiting to take us to the Western Sector of the city. Soon after, there ensued the usual harangue at the checkpoint. Because our government didn't recognize East Berlin, we had no visas to allow us in or out. But because we had diplomatic passports, they always let us through—not without lots of exchange. A number of times, enlisted personnel from the Embassy who did not have diplomatic passports were jailed for not having the visa. There would be *days* of "negotiations," and then finally they would be released.

We had rented an apartment in the American Sector of West Berlin, near the hospital, and through American friends there had arranged for a young German nanny to take care of the girls during our stay. She was in the apartment when we arrived, and when we mentioned how rough the flight had been, she told us we should never fear Soviet airplanes. Very seriously, she explained that because German pilots trained their Soviet counterparts, we had nothing to fear—German pilots were the best in the world! (Thanks a lot, Erika, but it took me a long time after that flight to get on a plane again, except for the Ambassador's American aircraft, which I did make use of when it was available.)

Anyway, the next morning I took my medical records to the American Hospital, and while I was sitting in the doctor's office there and chatting with him, I coughed slightly and, as they say, "All hell broke loose." I was raining blood. I recall the horrified looks of the other young pregnant women sitting in the hall waiting their turn, as the doctor raced by them with me on a portable cot covered with blood.

Then followed two or three days of trying to stop the bleeding, during which, since it was evidently so bad, they sent in a priest to administer the Last Rites. I remember thinking: I'm too young to die, and I'm not going to let the priest administer to me—because, then, I *would* die. So I tried to be very glib, and said, "Hi, Father. How are you? Where are you from in the States?"

"I'm from Chicago. But never mind that, my dear. Do you want to make a confession? Please let me say these prayers . . . You're a very sick girl, and—"

"No, Father, please just give me your blessing and pray for me. I'm not about to leave this world at twenty-four years of age, and I'm certainly not going to leave it from West Berlin!"

The priest smiled and said he would be back later.

After that, I recall the two doctors, who were with me almost the entire time. One of them told me, later, that both of them were with me for seventy-two hours straight, and that if this had happened while I was in Moscow, I never would have made it. It turned out that the American Hospital had had to have flown in from Wiesbaden a drug called Fibrinogen, in order to stop the bleeding. (The two doctors, along with several others, had made a recent tour of medical facilities in Moscow, and, along with other recent Western advances in medicine, the drug Fibrinogen was unheard of there.)

But the best part—the beautiful, glorious end to this tale, which I didn't learn about until a week later—was that during the first ten hours of the ordeal, a broadcast went out over Armed Forces Radio in Berlin that a young American officer's wife from the Embassy in Moscow was in critical condition in the American Hospital from loss of blood, and that any donors of Type O Negative would be appreciated. I was told that hundreds of G.I.'s lined every hallway of the hospital and the outside walks for three days, offering their blood.

I still can't talk about it easily. I can hardly write about it without misting up. It was the most beautiful thing that has ever happened to me. There is something about serving your country in a foreign land that brings you close to your countrymen, makes you more proud of your fellow Americans. This gesture by so many generous, giving Americans still makes my heart burst with pride. It was the greatest example of Doing It Right that I have ever experienced. Right on, troopers!

CHAPTER VI

"IT'S A BIG, WIDE, WONDERFUL WORLD"

We all know how big and wonderful the World or Life really is but we tend to forget it when the plumber fails to show or one of those big, wide (not too wide) wonderful guys walks out on us. But there are other plumbers, other guys. What we must remember if we are Doing It with Style and Grace is *never* to lose that precious thing—the intangible that saves us in most negative situations—our Sense of Humor.

I'll never forget the night Anna Chennault had a housewarming party in her just-finished penthouse apartment in the then-new Watergate complex here in Washington, D.C. Anna—the beautiful Chinese wife of the late General Claire Lee Chennault (of Flying Tigers fame), journalist, author, presidential appointee and business executive—was hostessing a party for much of official Washington, some of the social set and a squadron of those aging but dashing Flying Tigers. We weren't long into the party when blobs of water began descending on the coifs of the ladies, the distinguished greys of the generals and Anna's exquisite Chinese antiques.

Impossible! The roof of the spanking-new Giuseppe Cecchi–designed, world-renowned Watergate was dripping not only on the heads of Cabinet members, senators, congressmen, Tigers and their ladies, but on Oriental objets d'art hundreds of years old. All of a sudden, maids were scurrying about with Ming and Meissen bowls, placing them strategically to catch the water. Obviously, the situation could have put a damper—a Real Damper—on the party, but Anna and everyone else thought it quite hilarious that this slick, new, gleaming, potentially historic building had a leaking roof before its first birthday. Anna could have pouted and stamped her feet and gone on about how unfair life is but she knew that fact is a given. So she Did It with her usual Style and grace and just glided around the Ming and Meissen, offering her usual Pearls of Wisdom, gracious hospitality and delightful sense of humor. "Did you ever hear of it raining on an inside parade?" she asked. That sense of humor carries Anna far.

So, all of us who are Doing It with Style and Grace will remember that there is a light, Up side to almost any Down situation. The truth of that was forced on me some years ago when we were having a cocktail party and the bartender never showed. But Tongsun Park, long before he got in trouble with the government, did show. With his then avant-garde stretch limo (the adjective wasn't even attached to cars then) stashed carefully at the front door (never known for subtlety, that Tongsun!), he marched in resplendent in his double-breasted white suit, white shirt and white tie. This was a couple of years before the movie *The Great*

Gatsby was released and No One was wearing what my father used to call "an ice cream suit."

Tongsun must have noticed my semi-frantic expression and Mike, my husband, racing about taking drink orders. I told him why and he immediately took over, standing at the bar with all the graciousness of his Korean ancestors, asking each guest what he humbly could mix for him or her. Everyone was completely taken with his Oriental charm and especially his early Gatsby attire. By the end of the evening, both Tongsun and I had many requests for his services at upcoming parties whose hosts wanted the newest, eclectic bartender in town. Alas, Tongsun, however graciously, had to turn them all down. He had other matters to attend to.

Alors, mes chers, you do get the point. No matter how bad you think the situation is, if you sharpen up your sense of humor and remember that there's almost always an Up Side to the Down, you come out triumphant in the end. It is called Doing It with Style, Taste and Humor, which is what we are striving for. And, please don't think for a minute that I view the absence of a bartender as a National Tragedy. It is just une petit illustration of how you (or someone like Tongsun) can take things in hand when they seem out of control.

On the other side of that vignette, let me tell you a tale of how you never, ever want to Do It—the complete reversal of everything we believe in and have seen work so well. Not that we need any negatives, but quite often they do make the point.

Remember the former Miss Philadelphia I spoke of in the chapter "The Way You Wear Your Hat"? The former Miss Philadelphia, who we will call Barbara because that *is* her name, has been Doing It since copping the title, by heading up her own company on the West Coast. It has nothing to do with beauty or exercise as you might expect, but rather it's a unique answering service for celebrities in Hollywood. She hires only British men and women who have distinctive, upper-upper voices to answer the phones of the stars. The service costs twice as much as the ordinary ones (most of which reply with a banal, "Yeah, I'll tell 'em") and always has a long waiting list. So we get the picture. Barbara has been Doing It Right most of her life. She looks as great now as she did when she won her title, maybe better, and she thought of a unique gimmick that changed an ordinary business into a smashing success.

I met Barbara crossing the Atlantic to Europe on the *Queen Elizabeth II* one summer when I was going through my Fear of Flying crisis. No, not the Erica Jong version, but rather a real fear of boarding an aircraft. Too many near-catastrophes flying in and out of Russia probably did it, and skidding into a hangar after landing on ice in Warsaw finished me off for a few years. So, although Mike would accompany me one way across the ocean, he would fly the other. Ten days in transit is too long for a busy surgeon. I finally took Pan Am's Fear of Flying course and have been winging it ever since.

But, back to Barbara. We met the first night out to sea when the maitre d' urged me to sit at a table of single people traveling alone, even though I really wanted a table to myself. He told me I could have that the next day if I wanted it but he believed I would enjoy the group more. He was right, of course. I never did get all that reading done that I was looking forward to while at sea—but I did have a lot more fun. Barbara immediately told me she had seen me boarding that afternoon and had loved my big white oversized sailor hat. I recalled that she had on a stunning beige outfit with a wonderful little matching cap. In fact, we were both among the very few who wore hats as the ship pulled away from the dock in New York with the passengers throwing paper streamers and confetti to the crowd on the dock as the music played and the ship emitted several ear-shattering blasts.

We had a great crossing, with the three single men at our table and a couple at other tables in hot pursuit of Barbara and me all over the *Queen Elizabeth II*. We went swimming, dancing, gambling and we dressed to the nines every night for the black-tie dinners which are truly as fine as in any of the greatest restaurants in the world. (Don't ever confuse a Caribbean cruise with crossing the Atlantic on the *QEII*, or the *France* or the *United States* when they were under way. Different as day is to night. If you really want to Do It with Style, go first class on the *QEII* while it is still making the Atlantic run.)

Barbara and I became good friends after that trip. We met again in Paris and later that year she came to visit me in Washington. I even gave her one of my paintings that she fell in love with. Barbara was not exactly a major art critic but it still is very exciting when someone reacts so positively to your work.

I mentioned that we were going skiing. She had never skied, and so I told her of people, mostly Europeans, whom we would meet in Kitzbühel who also didn't ski and thought we were crazy to Do It. Imagine! Anyway, they would walk, take sleigh rides, ice-skate and drink in the fabulous mountain air. Plus, they were champions of après-ski and I told Barbara she could do likewise.

Off we went to Kitzbühel and were there just a couple of days when Barbara met an enchanting guy who had literally picked her up from the icy mounds on the bunny slope.

Barbara was so excited, she immediately called our room and said, "Wait 'til you meet him. He's an architect, a partner in one of the greatest architectural firms in the world. Lives in San Francisco. Is divorced. Is Divine!"

Well, we all met for drinks and Barbara was right—he *was* divine. Tall, dark and handsome, with an easy, affable charm you couldn't resist, John was THE famous partner in a prestigious firm, a Doer of note and comparably modest to boot. He was traveling alone and was scheduled to leave the next day but was so intrigued by Barbara he stayed for another few days until we were leaving for St. Moritz.

We had no sooner checked into our rooms at the incomparable Palace Hotel in St. Moritz when we received a call from Barbara in her room on another floor. "You won't believe it! My room is swamped with flowers, wine and chocolates. And guess what? John is here. He postponed whatever he was going to do in New York and followed me here!" Barbara was close to delirious. "He wants to meet us all in the bar before dinner. He's out skiing. So I'm going to start gussying up right now. See you later. Don't be late!"

Every night at the Palace Hotel is black tie and the gowns and jewels of the women there are not to be believed. Every night is like a contest to see who can out-designer and out-jewel the rest. The afternoon tea and musicale (yes, I said musicale) in the magnificent, marble-pillared lobby are, however, my favorite Palace Hotel Happenings. Every international movie star, orchestra conductor, opera star, society figure, politician, TV anchor, high-priced "companion" and notorious jewel thief that you have ever imagined parades through that breathtaking room from four to six in the afternoon. The music is playing softly in the background, glasses are clinking (tea is not the only beverage served), the unscheduled fashion show commences: All-white ski suits with matching boots, of course, fur parkas of every denomination, all-black stretch suits (once highly favored by Leonard Bernstein), lemon yellow and neon-orange jump suits, usually glued to the nymph-like "companions of the famous," and so much more that you are dazed, if not dazzled. And, after drinking all this in along with the tea or champagne, you stagger toward the elevators and lo and behold, there is the most glittering display of jewelry you will ever see in any hotel lobby in the world. Technically, it is in one of the wide-open, fifty-by-thirty-foot rooms off the main lobby where a distinguished white-haired gentleman from either Cartier, Van Cleef, or Boucheron displays the "faintable" jewelry. One early evening as I was schlepping up to our rooms with my husband I decided to "just look" at the display. An older man with a starlet-type companion was asking the price of a dome-shaped ruby ring. "That's four-fifty," the d.g. (distinguished gent) replied. "O.K.," replied the portly older man, "send it up to 212." As the atypical couple sauntered out, it dawned on me that the price was not $450 (that would buy a gold chain at Van Cleef) but rather $450,000! After we had inquired about a couple of dazzlers, the d.g. told us he could send anything we liked up to our rooms where we could make up our minds at leisure. (That's the old "take-it-home-and-try-it bit" that works ninety percent of the time with art, clothing, furs, whatever.) I asked the d.g. how did he know we weren't jewel thieves? How could he risk that? He replied, "First of all, we know most of the notorious jewel thieves and their ruses and, secondly, we have inconspicuous guards all over the hotel. For a finale, we are so heavily insured that we can take the risk."

What he didn't say was that one of those guards would, inconspicuously, follow you up to your room to see that you didn't suddenly leave the hotel. I wanted to say, "Send everything I laid my beady little eyes on up to the room." But I controlled myself and was generously rewarded an hour or so later when the d.g. appeared at our door with the gorgeous gold and diamond bracelet I had drooled over, accompanied by a note from my husband that rivaled Charles MacArthur's famous quote when he first met the young Helen Hayes. They were at a cocktail party in New York, the aspiring young playwright and the beautiful young actress. Charles took one look at lovely Helen, passed her a dish of peanuts and said, "I wish they were emeralds!" But, I digress. However, you do get the mood, the ambiance at the great old Palace Hotel.

Later that night we did all meet in the bar and, let me tell you, old Barbara, who had been Doing It Right for most of her life, outdid herself this time. She didn't rush off to the beauty shop either. She washed her own hair, rinsed it in that age-old gleamer, beer, gave herself a facial with a little never-advertised tube you buy in the drug store, did her exercises to put some natural color in her cheeks, and overdosed on bath oil and softener. O.K., so she wasn't out on the slopes. But she made up for all of that by opening the windows to get that intoxicating air into her lungs. She was Doing It for herself in her own way, which is what she'd always done.

I have to say there wasn't an actress, diva, starlet-companion in the room that could touch her. The ash-blond hair gleamed, the skin glowed, the smile electrified, and the bod that won her the "Miss Philadelphia" title still as good, if not better, was sheathed in a stunning pale violet silk gown. And, are you ready for this? John had called and asked what color she was wearing and had selected a pair of amethyst and diamond earrings delivered to her by our d.g. from Van Cleef. (He certainly had a busy night that Tuesday.)

Yes, Barbara had John completely enchanted. Enveloped in fur blankets, they took rides across the frozen lake in a sleigh pulled by two magnificent horses. They had hot chocolate at one of the many cozy Swiss tea shoppes every day. John would even watch her progress on the bunny slopes when he finished his daily runs. Then one night It Happened! Barbara undid everything she had been Doing Right.

John had asked Barbara, ourselves and a few other guests for caviar and champagne in his rooms before the evening ritual of people-gown-and-jewelry watching in the bar and at dinner. Barbara had arrived early to help arrange flowers and things before the others arrived. John was in his room taking a long-distance call. On a side table, as related by Barbara, she saw a telegram lying open with the message: "Miss you stop; love you stop; when will you be home stop. Anne." Well, Barbara was furious. Despite the fact that she knew John was divorced, she seemed to think there was no one else in his life, which was a ridiculous assumption, being as attractive, successful and especially as very nice as he was. I tried to tell her this to no avail. She got through the party but the vibrations were so bad that Herbert von Karajan, the late great conductor, excused himself early. Who can pick up vibrations better than a symphony conductor? And, believe it or not, that was the end of the affair, despite John's

pleas, along with mine and everyone else who thought she
was Doing It badly.

Later in the year, John called her from San Francisco a
week before her birthday and arranged to fly down on that
day and they had dinner together. The fact that he remembered the day, brought her another lovely gift and was his
usual charming self didn't budge Barbara. That was the last
time she saw him and I will never understand it. It is a master
lesson in not Doing It Right!

There was another Barbara incident that so infuriated
me I have never seen her since. It was another ski jaunt, this
time to Aspen, Colorado. This was our first trip to Aspen
and a good friend and super interior designer here in
Washington was going with us. Neil grew up in the West, was
a marvelous skier, and was excited about showing us his part
of the country.

We met Barbara at the lodge in Aspen as arranged and,
after a brisk tour of the town, had a wonderful dinner at one
of the many fine restaurants in town. We were ready to go
to some of the night spots that Neil knew so well when
Barbara decided to go back to the lodge pleading exhaus-
tion.

The next morning she called me to say she was furious.
"Why didn't you tell me Neil is gay?" she asked. "How dare
you bring him as a date for me?"

I had a feeling that was what bothered her and I was
equally upset at her for acting so stupidly.

"First of all," I told her, "it never entered my mind that
his being gay would matter at all. Neil grew up out here,
he's a great skier and wonderful company. I thought he'd
make a perfect escort for you during our après-ski rounds.
And another thing, Barbara, you were inexcusably rude to

him and to us last night when it dawned on you that he *might* be gay. I'm very disappointed in the way you're behaving."

Barbara calmed down a bit at this but added, "Well, I can't help the way that I feel."

We hung up and made no plans to meet later that day or any other. But that night in one of the "Western saloons" so favored in Aspen, there was Barbara smooching away in a corner with a very good-looking guy who was at least ten years younger than she.

She waved happily at us, not the least bit embarrassed as she introduced "Gary" to the three of us.

The amazing thing was that, although we saw Barbara almost every night out of the following ten, she was only with Gary one other time but every other night with a new man, invariably younger, a couple of them possibly in their late teens.

Obviously, Barbara had a youth thing going even though she wasn't *that* old. Early forties seems to be the time that the preference for the VERY YOUNG explodes in many men and some women. Here was a woman who was Doing It so well in so many ways but when it came to the men in her life she wanted only youth and variety. How many women do you know who would toss away a leading international architect like John M., who believe me was an eight on a scale of one to ten, who obviously adored you, for one night flings with just-past-pubescence males?

Our point here, *mes amis*, is obvious. We all have our weak spots, our vulnerabilities, our disappointments. And even when we are Doing It so well in many ways, we can fall down and stumble in another area. What we have to do is recognize the weakness, address it, not let it take hold. After all, if we are Doing It so well in so many other ways, we *must be* pretty strong, pretty bright, *n'est-ce pas*? If, like Barbara, we have the smarts in so many ways but realize we are not Doing It Right in another way, we correct that, overcome that. You will feel so much better about yourself. And that, as you know by now, is what this book is all about.

To lift us up after that negative bit, let me tell you a very positive Doing It story about one of my favorite actors, James Garner.

Actually, there are two stories that evolved when he was shooting a segment of the mini-series "Space" in our house in Georgetown a couple of years ago. My husband and I had to be convinced by Paramount Pictures that there would be no damage and that everything would be insured, if we agreed to let them film the picture there. They had seen the outside of the house and it was just what they wanted, and, please, could they come in and see if the interior was also what they wanted. It was. And they did convince us.

They were going to film a scene of the senator (Jim Garner), who in the movie pushed the space program through Congress, coming down the stairway into the main hall. Then he goes into the library where he has an argument with his wife (played by Susan Anspach). The doorbell rings and it's the senator's Girl Friday (played by Blair Brown). The senator escorts her in and later out again.

There were numerous conferences with the Paramount advance people, the District of Columbia Film Location people and like that. Eventually, the hot July day of the shooting arrived. There had been a write-up about it in the *Washington Post* the day before. Consequently, every woman I have ever known, seen and never ever heard of called to see if they could watch the filming—the scenes with James Garner, specifically. I narrowed those requests down to about twenty-five. Outside, the District Government had closed off our street to traffic. The catering company for the film—they follow to every location, I learned, to insure against any ills from strange foods in different areas—set up long picnic tables in our courtyard for the cast and crew. Then, there were the special effects people there to make rain to set the mood for the ominous scene to be filmed in the library later as Susan Anspach and Jim Garner have a knock-down, drag-out by a library window facing the street. When the Rains Came, I'm told, the hundreds of people assembled outside broke into spontaneous applause and cheers. Among those spectators were many of our Large-on-the-Political-Scene neighbors. Included among them was General Godfrey McHugh, JFK's military aide and, at that time, frequent escort of Jackie O., who this day assembled his wife, children and friends on lawn chairs across from our house with picnic and drinks at the ready. Our politicos and the Hollywood crowd have a great rapport. After all, they're both Doing It!

Back *inside* the house there were at least fifty people rushing around—electricians, decorators, cameramen, grips, gofers, plus my contingent of Washington women friends. Then Susan Anspach and her mother arrived, as ill-tempered as she comes off on the screen. Then the delightful Blair Brown, exactly as warm and friendly as she appears on film. There must be some truth to the old cliché that the camera never lies!

And then—and then—in walked the estimable James Garner. He moved directly through the throng right over to me and said, "You've got to be Dorothy." Now, I had never met him before and had only dealt visually with two advance people from Paramount who must have amazing powers of description. I wasn't doing a Glamorous Hostess Number either. I just had a T-shirt and white slacks on but he knew me right away. There was the loudest concurrent sigh I have ever heard as he effortlessly beamed into the room. "And I know who you are, too," I ventured.

Wong, our elderly houseman who had served many well-known personalities in his time and had never ceased to be absolutely inscrutable about it, finally lost his cool. "That's Maverick! I know him from long time. He my best!" Wong was delirious, even as delirious as my twenty-five friends who all seemed to be swallowing hard and licking their lips in unison.

The director called for silence as he described the first scene to big Jim, Susan A. (and her mother) and Blair Brown. The wife (Susan A.) was supposed to run down the semi-circular staircase, cross the center hall into the library with the senator (big Jim) following her down into the library, where, standing by the window, they have a Big Confrontation. The doorbell rings, Girl Friday (Blair B.) and possibly, at this stage, Something Else to the senator arrives and they have a discussion in the hallway. After she leaves, the senator goes back into the library and a violent argument ensues as the manufactured rain pelts the windows.

They rehearsed that scene several times. After the wife verbally tears into the senator, big Jim would come back into the hall where the army of onlookers were gathered and announce, with a big grin, "Wow, that's some beetch!" Each rehearsal elicited another Garnerism. "Ouch, she knows how to hurt a guy." A different comment every time was delivered to the onlookers with that famous smile.

After three or four rehearsals, the set decorators decided
our paintings going up the stairwell, all done in the sixties,
should be replaced with ancestral-looking portraits or at
least something done before the forties, which was the time
frame of the movie. They had a stash of paintings of every
period in one of the vans outside. So everyone took a break
while the decorators switched the abstract-expressionists for
some somber-looking founding fathers.The food caterers
outside were set up for three meals that day in the courtyard,
including coffee and noshes whenever the cast or crew
wanted them. Big Jim, however, was sitting talking to Mike
and me when Wong, in his everyday uniform of slippers
and starched white jacket, asked, "Mr. Maverick, you like
some coffee? I get." Although it was blistering hot and he
had just finished two Cokes, Mr. Maverick said he would love
some. Wong probably thought that because Mike and I
prefer coffee to almost anything else, it would be the best
treat he could offer his hero, especially the way Wong
brewed it.

When Wong returned with the silver tray and the best
china and placed his offering before big Jim, that wonderful
guy observed Wong's slightly bent frame, grey hair and
deeply lined face and raised himself from the depth of his
chair, bowed deeply and said, "I thank you, sir." Wong
returned the gesture with an even deeper bow and the only
uninscrutable smile I have ever seen him offer. That is what
I call Doing It with Taste, Style and Everything Else.

The other example of how this gentleman is Doing It the
Right Way all the time involves animals, a subject dear to my
heart. As I may have mentioned before, we get many requests to have benefits in our home. We used to give in to
many of the organizations that either my husband or I am

involved with—medical groups (his), musical, ballet, animal welfare and, of course, museum and art groups. It got to be too much. So now we limit benefits at home to either art or animal fundraisers, as they are the two most important things to me next to my family.

Anyway, as big James and I were sitting on the patio much later that day—Mike had gone back to the hospital and his patients—James G. heard our dogs barking. He asked what kind they were and I told him: an Afghan, a standard poodle, a springer spaniel and a mixed breed. I told him they were on the other side of the garden next to where we were seated—an almost block-long dog run which came with the house as if predestined for us. Then this big, warm, unpretentious "movie star" told me how he and his wife loved dogs and had several. The previous year he had inadvertently hit one of them as the dog ran under the wheels of his car in their driveway. The vet advised him to put the dog to sleep as all four legs were broken along with other injuries. Big James said he couldn't do it and then told his wife he would sleep with the dog downstairs in the maid's room until the animal could fend for himself. And so for five months he carried the dog outside several times a day and at night, feeding him by hand for almost as long. At first he said he thought it was guilt that made him do it, but he realized soon after it was because he loved the dog so much. His wife wasn't too happy with the situation but realized, too, that the dog's life and well-being meant more than any inconvenience.

I would call that Doing It Right, wouldn't you? And you don't have to be an all-out animal lover as I am, or obviously James Garner is, to realize that either.

Meanwhile, my Very Interested chums were peeking through the windows and doors to the patio the entire time this conversation took place. "Whatever were you two talking about all that time?" several of them asked. When I replied that the conversation was about dogs, most of my friends either looked skeptical or countered with, "Oh, I'll bet!" I just shrugged and gave them a Garner-like smile.

Every one of my women friends, as well as the men, were smitten with the affable aura of James G., and it wasn't that most of us hadn't been exposed to a number of opera, ballet and movie stars at many private parties in New York and Washington. But none of them that they or I had ever met had the natural charm (and I emphasize natural) that big Jim has.

One of my chums, Aniko Gaal, the fashion director and vice-president of Garfinckel's here in Washington, was completely overwhelmed by him. She had taken time off on a particularly busy day to watch the filming and, of course, the Star. He was a particular favorite of hers to start with but after she spoke to him and watched him work, she was a goner. Aniko noticed that on this particularly hot day, along with the makeup people blotting him with tissues after each take, J.G. had consumed a number of Cokes. When she had to leave, Aniko, normally the Coolest of Cool, blushingly asked if I would save her one of the Coke cans that big Jim had discarded. Now, Aniko has an international set of friends and escorts, spends part of her life in Paris, Brazil and New York, and is, as I mentioned, the epitome of COOL. But, as I also mentioned, she, like most of us, was sincerely smitten. So, of course, I said I would save a Coke can for her and even a few blotting tissues which she suggested as she raced out the door.

I couldn't believe her requests but I could understand them. So, after laughing about it that night with my husband, we decided to take one of the least dented cans (Mr. Maverick did a macho number with those cans!) and have it put on a small base, encase it in Plexiglas and have a small plaque placed on it. I took the Coke can to my super-fine framers here in Georgetown, who are used to rather zany requests from me, and they did a beautiful job, right down to engraving the plaque.

It sits now in Aniko's high-fashion office—a dented, aluminum coke can on a wooden base, sheathed in Plexiglas about two feet high and bearing a handsomely engraved plaque which reads

JAMES GARNER'S CAN
"SPACE"
1985

The blotting tissues float gracefully around the base.

CHAPTER VII

YOU GOTTA HAVE ART . . .
OR *SOMETHING* WONDERFUL
IN YOUR LIFE

You do agree, *mes chers*, you MUST have SOMETHING Wonderful in your life, and you CAN. You *must* realize by now that the passion in my life is ART (next to my family), seconded by Animals. But we are talking about your life, and the only reason I strongly urge that your passions be akin to mine is that there is nothing as rewarding, as ongoing and as never-ending in joy and discovery as art and the love of animals. But, if these are not for you, start Doing It—become Passionate about Something. Now!

Perhaps it's Music. Take Alexander Schneider (Sasha to his colleagues and fans), one of the Kennedy Center's Honorees in 1988 and one of our greatest chamber music violinists and conductors. When he was very young, he organized the first Casals Festival in Prades (France) in 1950. John and Jacqueline Kennedy came—they were just married. Years later, they invited Sasha to the White House (it was Jackie's love of chamber music, one of her many passions, that did it). The historic concert in 1961 was recorded and became a best-selling album. *Time* noted, "It might as well have been a concert led by Haydn at the court of the Esterhazys." There was a boom in the sixties of new chamber groups and recordings, all due to the famed Budapest String Quartet's concert at the White House with Sasha on the violin.

Alexander Schneider began studying the violin at five years of age. When he left Russia, Germany was the music center of the world and his father wanted him and his brother to become musicians. His father was a locksmith. And here's the part I love best: his father played the flute—very badly. "But," as Sasha says, *"he loved music. My, how he loved music."* Obviously, he was passionate about music and inspired by it, and he instilled in Sasha and his entire family that passion and inspiration.

So you see, my darlings, you can love something passionately and not have the talent of a Sasha Schneider, a Picasso or a Sarah Bernhardt; like Sasha's father, you can be Doing It simply by loving it.

Alexander Schneider's musicianship and his joy in it has inspired the New York Philharmonic, the Boston and Chicago Symphonies, the Philadelphia Orchestra, the Metropolitan Opera, and the New York City Ballet, to name just a few. Quartets in Tokyo and around the world feel his influence. Ever passionate about his music, Sasha's still Doing It at eighty.

Another music story concerns one of Washington's most flamboyant, beloved characters. Maria Fisher is president of the Beethoven Society, a group which has several concerts and parties every year. No, you don't have to play an instrument; a love for or a curiosity about Beethoven is enough. The indefatigable Maria, spry at eighty-five, goes to any lengths to recruit new members. But she outdid even herself a couple of years ago when she decided to have a Pisces party to attract new members. Being a Pisces herself with the coincidental name of Fisher, she thought it would be great fun to call almost everyone in the Washington telephone book with a "fish" name to come to the party. And call them she did: Admiral and Mrs. Fish, Mr. and Mrs. Thomas Cod, Henry and Alice Haddock, several other Fishers, Terry Shrimp and, my favorite, Mark Mussel. About forty "fish" people came to the party, loved Maria (who once sang with the Covent Garden Opera Company and who favors us with a few arias when anyone asks), and every one of the Pisces people became members of the Beethoven Society.

So there's Maria Doing It Right for eighty-five years and Doing It so well the District of Columbia government declared it Maria Fisher Day on her eightieth birthday.

She usually hauls a bust of Beethoven around with her and because of her years, certainly not because of physical capabilities, she allows some gallant gentleman to tote it for her. One evening the venerable replica accidentally slipped from the hands of Maria's escort. "My bust was dropped," Maria wailed for weeks, cleverly making sure the story (and the quote) was recorded in our local gossip columns. She achieved exactly what she wanted with the Fish story and the tale of the bust: more publicity and additional members for the Beethoven Society. Music is Maria's passion; Beethoven is her true love.

Theater is another Grand Passion for many of us and I have a couple of theater-related tales to tell. When the musical *Annie* previewed at the Kennedy Center, we decided to have an opening-night supper party at our house in Georgetown after the show.

A friend of ours with the State Department's Protocol Office, Patrick Daly, called the afternoon of the party to ask if he could bring along his guest, Señora López-Portillo, wife of the then-President of Mexico who was conferring with our President Carter at the time. I said sure, as it was to be a buffet supper, very casual, and we would be very happy to receive the president's wife. The Washington newspapers had been running pictures and stories about Señora López-Portillo, who looked like a Wagnerian opera star with a mass of dark hair and a rather massive body to match.

When we arrived back at the house after the theater with all the guests raving about *Annie* and the fabulous show-stopping song, "Tomorrow," I heard a commotion in the hall. There, coming up the marble staircase was a seemingly endless mob of people led by Patrick and Señora López-Portillo and what turned out to be her daughter; daughter's fiancé; fiancé's father, mother and brother; second and third daughters; and Señora L-P's estimable mother. Wait! There's more. Behind them and moving up swiftly on the sidelines were what turned out to be the Mexican Secret Service detail. Nine of them. Yes, I said nine.

Then, outside of the house was a low siren-like sound which turned out to be Our Secret Service, dispersing themselves around the property. None of this went over too well with our four dogs. Three of them were running the length of the house in the basement, barking in chorus. The fourth was up in the hallway barking away at the Mexican Secret Service.

Introductions were made and drinks were fetched and served in the library and the living room where the score of *Annie* was being played by one of our guests and many others were singing or humming along. Those, that is, who were able to act as if nothing unusual was happening. The entire Mexican contingent, with Patrick dead center and madly translating, positioned themselves near the piano (but didn't join the song fest) and hotly debated something. It turned out to be when and where they were going to eat.

Meanwhile, Wong, our houseman, and one of the bartenders were sending no-need-to-decode messages about the Mexican Secret Service detail. I went into the inside hallway and there stood the Nine in a tight circle, each vehemently pantomiming someone holding a glass to the lips, or just shouting, "Drink! drink!" We asked Patrick to tell them that we could serve them *"Aqua! Aqua!"* but no Real Drink while they were working. This did not go over too well. Nor did the antics of Prunie, our fourth dog, who was still racing around their feet, circling desperately for a random nip—she who, heretofore, only smiled and schmoosed with any and all visitors. The threatening voices and manner of the guards made her act in a protective way. The Nine demanded Prunie be removed, which I did only because I was afraid they would boot her across the room. They looked poised to do that. The buffet supper was at last ready but not before Mother of Señora L-P refused to be served a plate by Rosa, the maid, who, helped along by waiters from the caterers, was dishing-up everyone at the dining room table. Mother of Señora allowed as how she would only sup if she could have "French service." That meant seating her at a smaller round table in the dining room, which also meant pushing aside a French still life of rare veggies and a bowl of fresh flowers that occupied the table before Mother made her advance. So, there she sat in solitary splendor—no, I take that back—solitary stupor (Mother of Señora had mucho champagne, as two waiters

fluttered about her and served her three or four separate
courses with three or four different wines. But who was
counting? Certainly not Mother. When she left much later
she went out practically airborne with the able help of the
Nine. The only thing the two Spanish waiters refused to do
for Mother of Señora was to don white gloves while serving
her. First of all, they didn't have any with them. Secondly,
I wouldn't lend them mine. Finally, there is just so much
you can do for your country even for the mother-in-law of
El Presidente.

Yes, it was a Night to Remember. Our Secret Service men
outside in the cold for hours, refusing even coffee while on
the job, while warm and toasty inside were their counterparts, demanding but not receiving tequila or equivalent
(one did mention "geen") and actually, after a while, humming along and tapping a few feet to the tune of "Tomorrow, Tomorrow" which I hoped would get there soon.

As long as we are talking about Theater, I cannot fail to
tell you the greatest Theater-related story I know. Actually,
there are two and the first one is the shortest.

Our daughter Missy was majoring in Theater Arts in
college when in the summer of her sophomore year she and
a group of her fellow students went to London to study at
the Drama School of Rose Bruford. Soon after their arrival
the formidable Rose took her American charges on a bus
tour of London's theater district and everything related to
it, including the actors' favorite pubs, restaurants, et al. She
was saving the best for last. Her good friend, the actress
Constance Cummings, was performing with none other
than Sir Laurence Olivier in Eugene O'Neill's *Long Day's
Journey into Night*. Miss Cummings had agreed, as a very
special favor, to have the small group of students come

backstage after attending the matinee and meet the great actor. Actually, the acknowledged Greatest Living Actor.

As a prelude to that and left to be the next-to-last treat of the day was the sight of the Old Vic Theatre. For theater students it was like the afflicted reaching Lourdes, Moslems sighting the Great Mosque of Mecca. Anyway, Missy said they were all yelling, singing and carrying on when all of a sudden the bus was stopped and Miss Rose dramatically raised herself from her seat and solemnly pronounced, "*THIS* is the Old Vic."

Missy said the instantaneous silence was so heavy you could slice it. It was reverent. This was where It All Started. No one spoke until they got off the bus a bit later to attend the matinee of *Long Day's Journey*. When they went backstage after the performance, Constance Cummings emerged from her dressing room, greeted the budding Thespians and good friend Rose enthusiastically, if a bit dramatically.

Miss Cummings implored the students not to speak to Sir Laurence. She would introduce them but, please, don't bother him with any idle chatter or, worst offense of all, any requests for autographs. This had been hammered into them by Rose Bruford all week long. After all, they were Theater-People-to-Be. Autographs and idle chatter were beneath them, and certainly beneath Sir Laurence. The students were to line up, shake Sir Laurence's hand and move on.

Well, the Big Moment arrived and there was the Greatest Actor of the Century, magnificent in his red velvet dressing gown, ready to be presented to the aspiring thespians.

"Oh, Sir Laurence," intoned Constance Cummings. "I would like to present the American students of Miss Rose Bruford's School of Drama."

"How nice," said Sir Laurence. "Yes, hmm, very nice," he added as the students each shook his hand, smiling and murmuring how honored they were or something to that effect. Then, a good friend of Missy's who preceded her in the line did it. He asked Sir Laurence if he would autograph his program. Sir Larry stepped back a little, put one hand on his hip and *roared*, "We would be here a *f u c k i n g* long time if I started doing that, wouldn't we?"

The rafters shook. So did the students. But sign it he did.

Incidentally, the group ended up with autographs from the entire cast, including Constance Cummings (after she recovered) and the wonderful character actor Ronald Pickup, whose surname has to be one of my all-time faves.

It took about a week for dear old Rose to forgive them, but she did, realizing, I'm sure, that all these students were really Doing It with a true love and passion for the Theater.

The last and most significant theater-related story was at a New Year's Eve party at Hal and Judy Prince's town house in New York.

Before we went to that sensational soirée we attended a dinner party that Marta and Jerry Orbach were hosting. Jerry was starring in one of Hal Prince's shows on Broadway. That genius of the theater, Hal Prince, had three hit shows running concurrently at that time.

We had met Marta and Jerry Orbach on what was one of the last runs of the fabled transatlantic liner *France* in the early 1970s. It was an even more spectacular trip than usual. A whole group of us, including Marta and Jerry, had gotten together the first night out and formed an "alliance" for the rest of the trip. The group included Irving Wallace, the author, and his traveling companion who shall remain nameless; Edsel Ford, fresh out of college, and his buddy and former roommate whose name I can't remember; and Bobby Short, who would play all our requests in the little bar that remained open all night.

The second day out, young Edsel Ford, reading the ship's passenger list, saw his name spelled "Axel" and had them reprint the entire list. Bearing the illustrious name of his beloved uncle, which unfortunately was also the name of an unsucessful Ford automobile, Edsel did not want a joke made of his name, which is what "Axel" sounded like to him. And, believe me, on that gracious ship they would have been more than happy to have reprinted any John Doe's name correctly, too.

It was a wonderful trip. I can still see Irving Wallace checking the little book carts they push around the decks every day, making sure his books were featured prominently. (They always were—he was a regular on the *France*'s trans-atlantic run.) I can also see him promising the debarkation officials tons of his books as a gift if they let him off the ship immediately in Le Havre. Edsel Ford counter-promised with an offer of a few Mustangs if they let him go first. Just kidding, of course.

It was great fun, but the best part was the friendship we have had ever since with Marta and Jerry Orbach. Marta was in the theater until she had her children and then had her own talk show in New York. She is one of the most clever, outrageous, people in the world. Ask her about anyone (almost) in the theater world, TV or movies—what's so and so really like—and her answer is usually standard. "He's a creep." Then she will back it up with legitimate reasons. For the legion of those she loves (and who love her), she will sing their praises to the skies.

Back to the New Year's Eve dinner. We arrived very late and everyone was seated at a large round table. Just about every guest was a well-known name. I remember John Dockery, one of the Jets star players (now a TV sports reporter in New York), and his wife, Ann. Because everyone else was introduced with his or her title, by the time we got down to the people who would be sitting next to us I made a remark that no one will ever let me forget. When Marta introduced an older lady as Mrs. Gallo I asked, rather sweetly I thought, "Are you in wines?"

Not exactly in wines. Mary Gallo turned out to be the mother of the late Joey Gallo, who had been gunned down in Umberto's Clam House in New York just a year or so before. When Jerry Orbach was making the movie of Jimmy Breslin's book *The Gang That Couldn't Shoot Straight*, Marta had become, in advance of the shooting, intrigued with the "technical advisor" of that film—none other than Joey Gallo. Just released from the slammer, as they say, Joey had a great deal of technical advice to offer the moviemakers. Marta, who sincerely felt that Joey Gallo had many talents not apparent to anyone else, introduced Joey to the theater crowd in New York at a couple of her Sunday-night soirées. They, like most of us, were intrigued by a real live character right out of *The Godfather*. Through Joey, Marta met his mother Mary, who was as colorful and funny as Marta herself.

At the New Year's Eve dinner, after I inquired about Mary Gallo's involvement with wines, she took one look at my husband Mike and answered, "No, we aren't in wines; but tell me, Michael, do you have any brothers? I have a lovely daughter right here whose poor husband 'passed away' a couple of months ago and she needs another nice husband."

As it happens, Mike does have several brothers—two were unmarried at the time—but he "got the picture" and mumbled something like "Not really."

Meanwhile, back at Hal Prince's house, the party was overflowing with theater people from every show on and off-Broadway by the time we got there. Judy Prince, Marta's oldest and dearest friend, sat Mary Gallo in a high-backed chair in the center of the third-floor hall so she could greet everyone coming up from the floors below and join in the fun. (She was in her late seventies then and not in the best of health.) There were three floors to the Prince's town house and entire casts of different shows were moving up and down.

The third floor was, however, where all the action was. The band was playing all the hits from the Hal Prince–Steven Sondheim shows and I remember telling Steven S. how I loved the song "Being Alive" from *Company* best of all, and that if I were ever really sick and down just hearing that beautiful lyric and gorgeous melody would heal me immediately. The only thing was that most musicians were not familiar with the song; I had requested it many times to no avail. "Well," said the fabulous Mr. S., "this band will certainly know it." We both went up and asked for the song. You're right. They didn't know it and Steven Sondheim and I had one big laugh.

I saw Mike talking very seriously with Woody Allen, who was dressed in black tie as were all the other men. Only Woody, however, wore white high-top sneakers with his. I asked Mike what they were talking about. He said, "I told Woody that Marta Orbach thought he was one of the sexiest men in New York."

Woody's answer was succinct: "I always knew Marta was disturbed and should be in full-time analysis."

Roaming about the party, the two handsomest (and nicest) men, next to Mike of course, were the actor Ken Howard and the mayor, at the time, John Lindsay. I'm not often thrilled but I must say I was when John Lindsay asked me to dance and then, later on, cut in twice. A glaring example of how Not to Do It follows. When I was back in Washington and telling a couple of women about that "thrilling" happening, one of them said, "Oh, Lindsay probably was paying you all that attention because you were from out of town." Sweet, wasn't she?

Actually, as the mayor had inquired and I had told him, I was a native New Yorker but living in Washington, D.C., at present. He said he thought I looked very familiar (no, he doesn't need that or any old line!) and that maybe he had seen me on a magazine cover. Very flattering, I told him, but not true, even though I had done a couple of covers a few years before (like almost twenty, when I was a teenager).

Flashback to seven or eight years ago. The scene is Deauville, France, my favorite spot on earth. Why? Everything about it is everything I truly love: art, animals (horses, in particular), glorious architecture, the ocean, scenic beauty. Just about every great French artist has painted Deauville's beaches, polo fields, Norman estates and its stunning casino. If not, they've done Deauville's sister city, Trouville, or Honfleur, or one of the other beautiful towns along the coastline.

It was there in the Deauville casino one evening that I literally bumped into Omar Sharif. I had pushed my chair back from the roulette table, silently signaling Mike to meet me in the bar when someone said, "Please, allow me." It was Omar drawing my chair back. Then he looked directly at me and said, "How *ARE* you? You're looking wonderful."

I wanted to say, "And so *ARE YOU*," but played it cool and replied, "Just fine, and you, too, I hope."

"Oh, yes," said the big "O" as we walked into the bar with him telling me he was there for the International Bridge Tournament and a little "turn" at the tables and the races which are run several times a week in August, alternating with the polo games. Just then, his date or wife (does anyone really care?) marched up to us and grabbed Omar's arm and dragged him off. Mike was not far behind.

Anyway, every year since, we have seen Omar Sharif at the races, in the casino, in the hotel lobby, on the elevator (never on the beach!) and have our "catch-up" conversations, as other people (always women) are trying to talk to him or pull him away. Yes, the big "O" is as devastating in person as he was in *Dr. Zhivago*!

Another fascinating character to us in Deauville is not a theater person but rather the owner of a charming cafe near the center of town. The first time we had lunch there, also about eight years ago, she was fussing over us with the fascination some French people have with Americans. (I must say here that I have almost never run into the rude, patronizing French that so many Americans talk about.) Anyway, she laughed when we said we had no cameras and that we preferred red wine to white. (You know what I think about that wimpy drink!) We chatted about how Americans are different from the French in so many ways and yet alike in so many others. There was something indefinable about her that made me wonder if she had been a member of the French Résistance during World War II. No, somehow that didn't fit. More probable (in my wild imagination) it was the Collaborators. Maybe it was her very short haircut. Although I have read that the women collaborators had their heads shaved, I *do* think it would have grown in after thirty some years! Maybe it was the way she stood—hand on hip, head thrown back with an almost mocking smile on her lips. Maybe it was her "friend-boy" who was her age, about sixty, but who changed every year. Maybe and most probably it was all the books I've read of that period and my fascination with it. I do love to "cast" people in these wild stories—real or imagined.

However, we christened her "Madame de la Collaborateur" (not to her face, needless to say), and a strange thing happened last summer. My daughter Missy, who loves the story I made up about the cafe owner, pleaded with me to take a camera this trip and take Madame de la Collaborateur's picture.

Well, we tried to do just that after being welcomed back and shown her new dog, a tiny poodle, and her new "friend-boy" (a little younger this time). But, when we asked her to pose for a picture, Madame d.l.C. jumped up, yelling, *"Non, non, pas de photographie!"* Quite hysterically, she pushed the toy poodle at me and then the "friend-boy," both of whom I have photographed for posterity, but no Madame de la Collaborateur. *"Jamais, jamais,"* she kept shouting. We are still wondering if maybe my imagination didn't go too far this time.

Just a little vignette from Deauville and, if I was right about Madame d.l.C., that is the way we never want to Do It!

A short story about another kind of passion in life involves another theater person, Johnny Saunders, the British actor and a friend of Marta's whom I had met in London. I had promised him that when he came to the States I would take him on one of my tours of the Hirshhorn Museum and the Kennedy Center.

That I did, and I even smuggled him into the Museum Snack Bar (for staff only) where he enchanted everyone he met. They're still talking about Johnny and that wonderful view of life that most Brits involved in the arts seem to have. (Not without reservations, as you will see at the Kennedy Center visit.)

This was a daytime visit and he loved the sculpture of JFK that commands the Grand Foyer. He also thought the cubes of crystal that form the chandeliers in the foyer, Norway's gift to the Kennedy Center, were most impressive.

"And what did Great Britain give?" asked Johnny. "The greatest gift of all the countries, I believe," was my answer, as I dragged him up the red-carpeted steps leading to the Opera House. Outside of that great hall is Barbara Hepworth's magnificent, abstract sculpture that was given by Great Britain to the Kennedy Center.

"THAT was our gift?" the shocked Johnny queried.

"Yes, John. Hepworth studied with Henry Moore and works much in the same style and is, probably along with Moore, one of the greatest living sculptors." (This was just before Moore died.)

"O.K.," Johnny said. "Now let's see what the Irish gave."

I took him into a reception room where a dazzling Waterford chandelier commanded the room. "I can't stand it," John shook his head. "The Irish went us one better!" I told him he was crazy; that the Hepworth was far the finer, more artistically valuable gift. "Buggers," replied Johnny. "They got us again!" So you see, even when you're involved in the arts, Doing It—acting, painting, dancing or just having a passion for them—you can still be off the track about certain things. Growing up biased in any way is wrong and hard to set right once in motion. Like the Irish and the English. To some people, that's a breach that will never be healed. And one of the oldest ones.

But, to get us on the track again—about having Art or Something Wonderful in your life, do remember that even the Rothschilds, who rose to the heights of international finance and power two hundred years ago, are still Doing It Right today. Not each and every one of them, to be sure, but you know that any of them could easily become that degrading term "idle rich" and rest on the Rothschild name forever more. As one of today's Rothschilds says, there's a family trait of being insatiably "*interested* and *curious.*" One of this generation's female Rothschilds has been given an Order of Merit by the Queen of England for writing a definitive book on insects. Yes, insects. Someone obviously has to be curious and interested in insects—even a Rothschild. Her father was the definitive flea expert. Whenever he heard there was plague anywhere, he rushed to the spot. He obviously sparked his daughter's interest in this field. No lolling about on yachts and using the word "bored" over and over again for these Doers.

One thing we must remember in having Art or Something Wonderful in our lives is that a work of art is *work*. No great masterpiece, no great symphony, and no great novel or play was ever easy to create. But the interest and curiosity that ignited the fire, the work, is richly rewarded upon completion with a feeling of fulfillment that is incomparable. Again, I don't mean we have to paint a *Mona Lisa* or write a *War and Peace.* Just being curious enough to investigate what makes each of them a masterpiece is enough for most.

Getting out and Doing It Right is admittedly a difficult step. Much easier to swing on the hammock and watch people on TV Doing It. But once you get into some of those courses that you like in your local universities your whole life will change for the better. (It's also a great place for meeting a lot of Doers. It's much better than the local bar for you singles. But then anything is better than the local bar.)

I can think of so many unique and wonderful happenings in my life that never would have taken place if I stayed home in the hammock. (Not that I don't like *that* once in a great while.)

One day back in the sixties I was particularly exhausted but had promised my young daughters we would go to the circus that Saturday afternoon. I was, at the time, women's advertising and fashion director of a chain of stores here in Washington and had had a particularly hectic week. It would have been so easy to let them play with friends, but I had promised. Off we went and were no sooner at the window of the arena to pick up our tickets when the man behind the window did a double take, rang a little bell, and a white-haired gentleman with a red boutonniere appeared, bowed, took my arm, said "they" were honored, and escorted the girls and me to the Presidential Box inside the arena. When we were seated, I tried to tell the gentleman I was not supposed to be in that box—but he wouldn't listen. "Please, just enjoy the show. You too, *Caroline*," he said to Missy, who did bear a faint resemblance to Jackie Kennedy's daughter. And I, truth be told, had been mistaken for Jackie herself before.

Anyway, the girls loved the clowns and tight-rope walkers and the ringmaster coming over to take a bow before them. I must say I began to enjoy myself, especially at intermission when my good friends, Pat and Jack Armitage, a Foreign Service couple I knew from our embassy in Moscow, came over to ask what I had to do to get those great seats. Never would have happened if I stayed in the hammock!

A few years ago I was in New York tracking down a painting for a client of mine (I have an art consultant/interior design business). Unbeknownst to me, *U.S. News and World Report* was taking a group cover picture on the corner of Madison Avenue and Fifty-seventh Street as the group and I were waiting for the light to change. A few weeks later I received a call from a friend who said, "Hey, I see you're on the cover of *U.S. News.* . . . Recognized you right away . . . you're the only one with a hat on!" My mind flashed back to my solo fashion covers in my teen-college years. "Couldn't be," I replied. "They wouldn't use one of those . . . Wait a minute, we have the magazine here." Sure enough, under the heading "Mood of America" was the cover picture of a group of people on a city street with moi stage center with my little man's fedora plopped on my head. Wonderful picture. Now, if I had stayed home in the hammock and given up on the painting—well, you know the rest.

When I was living in Germany with my ex-husband, who was studying at a top-secret American school there in Regensburg, I pursued my love of horseback riding and through that met one of my oldest and dearest friends, Princess Marina of Thurn und Taxis. I just knew her as Marina until after one of our rides together she asked me "back to the Palace." The Palace in town has five hundred rooms; the country Palace or Lodge has only three hundred and forty. She began coming to our parties, sometimes bringing her older brother, Johannes, now married to his fourth cousin, who I'm sure you have read about if you read *"W," People,* or *Time.* Marina was great fun. All the single lieutenants were after her. One in particular used to ask, "But what's her real last name?"

It was her parents who were so fine—so much like Marina. They must have had her in midlife because they were quite old (but, then, I was twenty-two, as was Marina). They, the old Prince and Princess, were strict Catholics and were horrified at what had happened to their country at the hands of Hitler and were known for their great strength in standing up to that maniac during those horrific times.

Anyway, what I loved most was that Marina evidently told her parents that at our parties the young people all drank martinis and things like that, not schnapps. So, the first time we went to the palace for dinner we had martinis of seven-eighths vermouth and one drop of vodka instead of the reverse. No matter. I've always been an atmosphere or ambiance person first and, there at the palace, it was heavy with both. Where else does a white-gloved footman stand behind each chair as you dine? Not even at a state dinner in the White House or 10 Downing Street. And the conversation! How much they loved America. How the old prince knew three of our presidents. And only when pressed would he admit that the Thurn und Taxis title is one of the oldest in Europe, dating back to the twelfth century. A superb experience, but if I hadn't a passion for horses and hadn't pursued it, I would never have met the lovely Marina or her family.

Then, at a White House party a few years ago, I was privileged to hear the sharp wit of President Ronald Reagan firsthand. I went up to him at the end of the evening after the crowd around him thinned out and said, "Mr. President, we are among the few people here from Washington and I'd like you to meet my husband, Mike." Just then, a very large, busty and gutsy lady had nearly pushed me over in reaching for the President's hand. "I hope this isn't your husband, Mike," the President said with a wink. Quick. Sharp. Bright. That was our ex-pres.

Then there was Peter Duchin. If I hadn't been working hard myself on a Washington Ballet fundraiser, I would never have been able to talk him into playing for practically nothing for the fundraiser in exchange for a promise to have him play for our twentieth anniversary party. And that he did. It was the greatest of parties, except even Peter didn't know Steven Sondheim's "Being Alive." Now that Streisand has recorded it, I'm sure everyone will be humming it soon. In a way, I hope not. Look what happened to "Send in the Clowns." As I'm sure you have noticed, that one has become almost the cliché that "Stardust" and "Feelings" are. Let me finish this lengthy chapter with two of the people I started the book with—the late Justice Abe and Carol Fortas. Abe Fortas used to gaze longingly at a lively Dufy watercolor of ours entitled *Three Musicians*. He said once, "Dorothy, you love Art the way I love Music." He was right. I give art the love and passion he gave to music.

One night, shortly after we moved to Georgetown, the Fortases invited us to dinner. They knew I was a docent at the Hirshhorn Museum and so invited Joe and Olga Hirshhorn, along with the then-Librarian of Congress Daniel Boorstin and Mrs. Boorstin. When dessert was served, Abe rose and proposed a toast. "To Dorothy and Michael," he said. "They have done and will continue to do great things for our nation's capital city. Dorothy in the arts and Michael in medicine. You're a great addition." I gulped, I hope noiselessly. Here were three of the biggies of our age and they were raising glasses to US.

All I can say is if we are Doing It, and I think we are, I hope it's been done well and will continue to be with Style, with Taste and with Passion.

CHAPTER VIII

DOING IT WITH "T" AND "S"
(Taste and Style)

To give you the technical definitions of both Taste and Style, I cite the *American Heritage Dictionary:*

Taste: The faculty of discerning what is aesthetically excellent or appropriate.
Style: A quality of imagination and individuality expressed in one's actions and tastes.

What do Taste and Style have to do with our subject matter? Well, you shouldn't have to ask! If you're really Doing It or about to when you finish this book, wouldn't you rather be Doing It with T and S than just plain Doing It? Of course you would! I have given you the textbook definitions but Taste and Style are more easily acquired by observing. Not just looking, but as I said before, my darlings, you must observe; drink it all in and have it REGISTER. When you see a room that knocks you out, have a meal that looks and tastes like heavenly ambrosia or see someone dressed the way you would like to—start Doing It immediately by mentally jotting down the ingredients that combine to give the room, the meal or the outfit, the Taste and Style that made you—and probably everyone else—notice.

T and S usually go together—although a person's home or clothing can be in what is known as "good taste" but not have any particular style. That term "good taste' usually implies safety. Like wearing the ubiquitous black dress or suit almost every time you go anywhere. By this time, I hope, you will be adding lots of cream or white jewelry or scarves to your blacks. Better yet, Doing It with simple but knock-out clear reds or the no-color colors—greige, beige, taupe, celadon, banana or cream. I don't care what color hair or skin you have, these colors are a zillion times more flattering than the deadly, I-don't-want-to-be-noticed, cleric-from-the-Middle-Ages Black.

To give you a glaring example of Bad Taste and No Style, I submit the true story of one of our well-known fashion designers. It was at a Reagan White House dinner for Canadian Prime Minister Brian Mulroney. All White House dinners honoring a foreign head of state are black tie as expressed on the invitation which means the women wear formal gowns. This particular dinner for our Canadian neighbors was particularly sparkling with Nancy Reagan in glittery brown and gold, Mrs. Mulroney in dazzling beaded purple and the Princess Salmah Aga Khan outsparkling just about everyone. One of America's best known fashion designers, Norma Kamali, wore—are you ready?—a navy blue, knee-length suit with short blue ANKLETS over sheer blue stockings. Was she kidding? Was this the only way she'd be noticed? When a reporter talked to her, she said, "I think the White House is one of the few places left in our world that floor-length gowns work. I don't

really know people who wear floor-length gowns. At this or
a wedding, it's O.K." Gee, thanks, Ms. Kamali, for that
pronouncement. Obviously you don't hang out with people
who wear floor-length gowns. But I would think you would
have SUSPECTED that a White House State Dinner would
call for a little extra effort—even a short formal gown—
rather than your navy blue suit with anklets, an outfit more
suitable for running down Third Avenue on a dark, rainy
afternoon. Something funky left over from Studio 54 days
would have been at least an attempt at style.

The reason Norma Kamali's outfit is such a flagrant
example of Bad Taste and absolutely No Style is that her
selection was so very inappropriate. It was like wearing a
formal gown to a baseball game. A prerequisite to Taste and
Style in any field is that the choice be Appropriate. You
would never fill a living room with bathroom furnishings,
would you? Well, it's the same thing as Kamali wearing—I
can't say it again or I'll be sick—an N.B.S. w/A's. The real
irony is that the next year Ms. Kamali introduced a group
of floor-length gowns in her line.

Another White House story that has to do with T and S,
only positively as opposed to negatively, has to do with the
First Lady. My husband and I were at a reception at the
Reagan White House, with Nancy Reagan looking particularly beautiful in a pale peachy coral dress and matching
coral earrings surrounded by diamonds. (You'll never
catch a savvy, chic lady like Nancy in unflattering, ubiquitous
black. That lovely coral peach, incidentally, is probably the
greatest flatterer of all colors in the world.) Nancy's earrings were so gorgeous that I almost gasped (but that, of
course, would be tasteless to do at the White House or
anywhere else). I mentioned to my husband how beautiful

I thought they were and how perfectly they matched her dress. He agreed and later as President and Mrs. Reagan were leaving the room, my husband leaned over to the First Lady and said, "Mrs. Reagan, my wife just loves your earrings." Now, at this time, there was a small rumble in the newspapers about Cartier, Tiffany and Harry Winston lending the First Lady jewelry to wear on State Occasions. A great way for the jewelers to show their wares—but the public didn't like it. Mrs. Reagan, as the President was trying to elbow her out of the room, stopped and very directly said, "Oh, I'm so glad she likes them. Ronnie bought these for me years ago when we were on a holiday!" Obviously, great taste. Definitely great style. Plus a sense of humor.

A few months after that incident at the White House my husband and I were having dinner at the Jockey Club, our favorite restaurant in Washington, and there was the First Lady a few tables away having dinner with friends. When she got up to leave, a few of the other diners rose to try to shake her hand or speak to her. Nancy gracefully outwitted them all, circled around them and stopped by our table, smiled and said, "How are you?" When people asked why she singled us out, I can only say she must have remembered the two jokers who inquired about her earrings at the height of Jewelrygate and wanted to show she was still being gracious about it. Taste and Style—she's got it.

Speaking of Nancies, I think it's about time we do a little Nancy Mitford–type list. Remember her U and non-U, Upper and not Upper Class? Only ours will, of course, be concerned with Taste and Style. Most of the things we have talked about will be listed here, but for heaven's sake don't take them too seriously. If you drive a four-door car—O.K.

No one is going to call the Taste Police. But, on the other hand, when Diana Vreeland had her maid clean and polish the SOLES of her shoes—that's when it is no longer Style—it is beyond foolishness.

A last example of Taste—and, I might add, a great compliment to me—was at the Plaza Hotel last month. My husband and I were having brunch in the Palm Court and an attractive, familiar-looking man passed, gazing and smiling right at me. I said to Mike, "That man is so familiar. Oh, it's Donald Trump!" He turned just then and said to Mike: "You have great taste!" I've always liked D.T.!

Above all, keep in mind that these are my personal opinions. They do not reflect the opinions of my publisher or editors. I know, along with everyone else, that convertibles, for instance, are more dangerous than hard-top cars. And that four-door cars are easier to climb in and out of if you want to sit in back. But this list is only concerned with the lines and look of a car. Whether or not it can go from zero to sixty miles per hour in four seconds is not a concern here. (And why anyone would care about that seems ridiculous to me, anyway.) The same thing goes for vacation spots. You may love Acapulco, for instance. I personally find it an extension of Miami Beach—brash and vulgar, as even St. Tropez has become. But the following are *my* choices of people, places and things that reflect a definitive taste and style. And those that definitely do not.

You will notice on the people list that some of them have departed this world, but their influence in the taste and style of our times was so great it will live on forever.

Doing It with
BAD TASTE—*NO STYLE*

Men who wear polyester suits, hand-painted ties, running shoes except when running, gold chains, ruffled shirts, colored dinner jackets, and short-sleeved-shirts—especially Hawaiian

Following every fad from alfalfa sprouts to Zen

"Decorating" your home and letting the decorator impose his/her style; lavish floral displays on your tables, suitable only for hotel lobbies; over-marbleized, over-mirrored and over-lighted bathrooms; having some good paintings and knowing nothing about the artist or his period; art that is only "pretty"; having either no library, or no books, or books chosen by the yard; having "rec rooms" instead, loaded with the latest electronic equipment

LeRoy Neiman; Julian Schnabel; Chagall, Dali and Miró prints in mass editions, which usually means poor quality and that the artist sold out

Any TV sitcoms; any program with a laugh-track; any program with Joan Rivers, Suzanne Somers or Pee-Wee Herman

Tammy and Jim Bakker

Painting by numbers, copying anything

Doing It with
BAD TASTE—*NO STYLE*
(continued)

All four-door cars unless you need the ease of getting in and out; all Cadillacs and Lincoln Continentals, except the pre–World War II classic L.C.; all Japanese cars, stretch limos

Bragging about your prowess in any sport and/or incessantly talking about it

Las Vegas, Miami, Acapulco, Monte Carlo, any of the Hamptons for day-trippers, most of the Caribbean

"If it feels good—do it" (motto of the sixties carried into the eighties—until AIDS)

The so-called National Museum of Women in the Arts

Madonna, Tony Curtis, Sylvester Stallone, Pee-Wee Herman, Suzanne Somers, the Brat Pack, Eddie Murphy, Bruce Willis, Prince, Michael Jackson, Vanna White and Barbara Walters (when they open their mouths), Molly Ringwald, Cybill Shepherd, Sean Penn, Teri Garr, Arsenio Hall, Sam Donaldson, Jackie Mason, Jerry Lewis, Elizabeth Taylor, Tony Danza, Al Sharpton, Leona Helmsley, Zsa Zsa Gabor, Ethel Kennedy, Ted Kennedy

Doing It with
TASTE

Men who wear navy suits or blazers every time they go out, with "nothing" dark ties

Never changing anything from hairdos to husbands—even if they are equally offensive

Having everything in your home match perfectly; having your home look almost exactly like most of your friends'; having an inoffensive landscape (probably a road-company Hudson River School) over your fireplace with matching Wedgwood vases flanking it

Fragonard, Ingres, Bierstadt, Rembrandt, Rubens, David, Da Vinci

Most PBS programs; NOVA, the Pallisers, etc.

Nancy and Ron

Painting florals or landscapes, especially on Sundays

Two-door dark Mercedes, Jags, BMWs

Tennis, Ping-Pong, soccer, croquet, brisk walks, "doing the rapids," golf

Doing It with
TASTE
(continued)

Sections of the Cape and New England, Palm Beach, Palm Springs, London, and "Bed and Breakfast" places and small inexpensive inns in all these places

"Less is more" (Bauhaus credo)

The Metropolitan, National Gallery, Boston Museum of Fine Arts, Kansas City Museum, Louvre, Hermitage, Pushkin Museum, Corcoran Gallery, Albright-Knox Gallery, Philadelphia Museum of Art

Doing It with
STYLE

Men who informally wear light-colored slacks with
great striped shirts (sleeves rolled up). For business or
dinner, dark suits—black, charcoal-brown or grey with
pale-colored shirts, white collar and small pattern ties
with a silk square of color in the pocket

Doing it by adapting the New—*only* if it suits you;
being avant-garde; setting your own Style

Doing It by mixing all the greats (which you know
from reading and observing) in furnishing and art even if
they are not original—the way you mix them is what *IS*
original; doing everything in one color—walls, rugs, slip-
covers; hanging an avant-garde painting next to an antique chair or table (both have great lines—so they relate);
selecting your own flowers and blooming plants—all in
the same color—massing them all together or perching
them everywhere

Those Duchamp brothers—Marcel, Raymond
Duchamp-Villon and Jacques Villon; Matisse, Picasso,
Vuillard, Magritte, Stella, Frankenthaler, Henry Moore,
Braque, Gris, Nadelman, Archipenko, Arp, Léger, Bran-
cusi, Agam, Boter, Kieffer

"60 Minutes," "Tonight Show," "Late Night" with David
Letterman

Ginger and Fred

Doing It with
STYLE
(continued)

Doing It with paints by experimenting with knives instead of brushes, mixing colors you only dream about; painting your feelings

Classic cars; any convertible old or new; Jeep Wagoneers; station wagons—the older the better

Skiing, swimming, polo, horseback riding, sailing, squash, billiards

Deauville, Cap d'Antibes, Baden-Baden, Biarritz, Dubrovnik, St. Moritz, Paris, Québec, Carmel, Charleston, New Orleans, Boston, San Francisco. Again, there are charming small hotels at suprisingly low rates in all these places. You can enjoy their style even if you are on a budget

"I love luxury. And luxury lies in the absence of vulgarity"—Chanel

The Museum of Modern Art, Hirshorn Museum and Sculpture Garden, Menil Collection, Phillips Collection, the Frick Museum, Maeght Foundation, Musée d'Orsay, Dahlem Museum, Berlin, Scaife Wing, Carnegie Institute Museum of Art, Chicago Art Institute

THOSE WHO ARE
Doing It
(or Did It)
with
TASTE/STYLE

Cary Grant, Fred Astaire, David Niven, Frank Sinatra, Chanel, Gloria Vanderbilt, Diana Ross, Diahann Carroll, Audrey Hepburn, Michael Graves, Valentino, Calvin Klein, William Buckley, Gore Vidal, Carly Simon, George Hamilton, Dudley Moore, Lena Horne, James Conlon, Leonard Bernstein, Steven Sondheim, Robert Redford, Arthur Mitchell, Robert Wagner, Roger Moore, Michael Caine, Robert Klein, Jack Nicholson, Tom Cruise, Sir Laurence Olivier, James Garner, Omar Sharif, Ben Bradlee, Katherine Graham, Arthur Colton Moore, Louise Nevelson, Tom Wolfe, Chuck Robb, Donald Trump, Robert Palmer, Lisa Sliwa, Jackie Onassis, John F. Kennedy, Jr.

Well, now you know—Doing It with Taste is simply practicing good manners, being conservative and always safe. Doing It with Style is always in good taste, never flamboyant and always going with your own personal touch. Remember what Oscar Wilde said: *"If you can't be a work of art, dress like one."*

And if we have learned anything about Doing It Right with diet, it is primarily that the AMOUNTS we eat are what make the difference in our waistline measurements. We can have eggs, meat, cream, salt—if we have no health problems—but again, the AMOUNT is always uppermost in our mind. Our motto for life is N.F.A. (With rare exceptions, of course.)

If we have learned how to Do It Right with our eyes, we will be able to recognize immediately why the little VW Rabbit convertible has more style than a Jag or Mercedes *sedan*, for example, and why Redford has it and Sean Penn doesn't.

And if you ever wear another nothing black dress because you believe that old rhubarb that it makes you look thin or chic—then you had better go back to the forties or fifties when grandma and that vintage fashion editor told you all those lies. O.K. Any dark color is going to make you appear a few pounds slimmer, but a glorious color or even a dark-dare-I-say-it-"black" dress accented with white, or gold jewelry (masses), or scarf, or shawl is going to make you look prettier, smarter, more socko, more chic. Would you trade in those glorious descriptions for that wimp of a word "thinner"?

And, if you are Doing It Right with your Eye—going to museums and galleries like mad—you're getting to be so hooked on Art that you will wonder why you threw away your life before when there was one of the Greatest Joys in Life—if not the Greatest—for the taking, absorbing and loving.

And most of all you're going to be Doing It Right with your Eyes in the most important way of all—reading. Not just those newspapers and magazines, but books. You don't have to go out and buy every bestseller that comes along. Start Doing It Right by reading reviews of the new books and requesting them in your local library Along, of course, with the classics to read or reread. And remember when we moved to our house in Georgetown years ago? Describing its location to an acquaintance, I said, "Along with the house being so fabulous, the Georgetown Library is right on the corner." She looked at me as if I were crazy. "As if you'll ever use that," she said, patting her bleached, teased hair-do. Actually, I extract at least a dozen books a month from that wonderful place (as is every library) and enjoy, absorb and learn from almost every one of them. I know I told this story before but it does make the Point so well.

If you are Doing It Right with Books, you will honestly feel as I have since reading *Anna Karenina* years ago. No film production has ever produced an Anna as beautiful as in my imagination; no costume or set could equal those I created in my mind. The pen of Tolstoy was so keen in its creation of atmospheric detail that I have never been in a train station where clouds of white smoke and haunting whistles don't remind me of Anna and the beginning and end of her story.

There has never, ever been any movie made that improved on a book, because with the movie's words and pictures, it is DOING, IT for you. Robbing you of your imagination—your power to DO IT RIGHT—create images yourself.

Of course, you know by now that Doing It Right with your life means not being mesmerized by TV. You are not spending a good part of your days on earth watching sports instead of going out and Doing Them, or watching soaps or sitcoms instead of creating your own interesting life. Remember Auntie Mame's bon mot about life: It's a Big Feast and most of us don't even go up to the table to nibble.

Speaking of the Feast of Life and Doing It Right, or missing out by being passive and not Doing Anything, the following remark illustrates everything I have tried to put down about Doing It Right and how some people can be told, exposed and even immersed and they still miss the point. About how most TV and films rob us and our children of all the very good things in life—if we let them. How films and TV are all words and pictures and leave nothing to the *IMAGINATION*. If we need any one thing to keep us Doing It Right, it is our imagination.

During the writing of this book, a friend asked me how it was going. I replied that finding the time to keep at it was the toughest part. "But then," I said, "it's not exactly *War and Peace*."

"Oh, yeah," she replied, "I saw that. Audrey Hepburn, wasn't it?"